Yugoslav "Self-Administration" - Capitalist Theory and Practice by Enver Hoxha
2011 Prism Key Press // www.prismkeypress.com

Yugoslav "Self-Administration" Capitalist Theory and Practice

Enver Hoxha

Contents

A great amount of publicity is being given to a book published in Yugoslavia last year by the leading theoretician of Titoite revisionism, Edvard Kardelj. It is called "Directions of the Development of the Political System of Socialist Self-Administration".

The anti-Marxist ideas of this book were the basis of the entire proceedings of the 11th Congress of the Yugoslavian revisionist party, which the Titoites, in an effort to disguise its bourgeois character, have named "League of Communists of Yugoslavia".

The Titoites and international capitalism propagate, as the 7th Congress of the PLA pointed out, the "system of self-administration" as "a ready made and tested way to socialism". It is serving as their favourite weapon in the struggle against socialism, the revolution and liberation struggles. Considering this danger, I thought it necessary to voice some thoughts about this book.

Capitalism has been fully restored in Yugoslavia, as is well-known, but this capitalism knows how to disguise. Yugoslavia portrays itself as a socialist state, but of a special kind, as the world has never seen it before! The Titoites even boast that their state has nothing in common with the first socialist state which emerged from the socialist October Revolution and which was founded by Lenin and Stalin on the basis of the scientific theory of Marx and Engels.

The Yugoslav renegades abandoned the scientific theory of Marxism-Leninism on the socialist state right from the beginning and have worked to prevent the establishment of the dictatorship of the proletariat, to ensure that Yugoslavia would proceed on the road of capitalism.

I have already explained at another occasion that the Titoite renegade group, which disguised itself and portrayed itself as followers of the socialist system established in the Soviet Union and which trumpeted that it would build socialism on the basis of the scientific theory of Marxism-Leninism, in reality both before and after the liberation of Yugoslavia was opposed to this ideology and to the Soviet revolutionary experience. This correct conclusion arises clearly from the content of Kardelj's book, too.

1. A Brief Excursion on the History of the Titoite Revisionists

The national liberation war of Yugoslavia under the leadership of the Communist Party of Yugoslavia embodied the courage and bravery of the people as well as the honesty of the genuine communists of Yugoslavia. During this struggle, however, certain dubious tendencies appeared within the Yugoslav leadership, which made one think that in its stand towards the anti-fascist alliance of the Soviet Union, the United States of America and Great Britain, the Tito group leaned towards the Anglo-Americans, which became quite clear later. At that time, we observed that the Titoite leadership maintained very close contacts with the Western allies, especially with the British, from whom they received extensive financial and military aid. Likewise the obvious political rapprochement between Tito and Churchill and his negotiators became obvious, at a time when the national liberation war of Yugoslavia ought to have been closely linked with the liberation war of the Soviet Union, since the hope of all peoples for the all round liberation, as far as the external factor was concerned, rested at precisely this war.

The tendencies of the Titoite leadership, which aimed against the Soviet Union became more evident on the eve of the victory over fascism, when the Red Army, in hot pursuit of the German army, entered Yugoslavia to assist the national liberation war there. Especially at the time when the conclusions of this great war were being reached among the great and small states involved, it became obvious that Titoite Yugoslavia had been supported by British and US imperialism. At that time, the diplomatic and ideological frictions between the Soviet Union and Yugoslavia grew more evident. These frictions were, among other things, over territorial questions. Yugoslavia claimed territories in the North, especially on its border with Italy. But it was silent about its southern borders, especially its border with Albania, about Kosovo and the Albanian territories in Macedonia and Montenegro. The Titoites could not speak about this, because they would have violated the chauvinistic platform of the Serbian nationalists.

Today it is common knowledge that the differences between the Yugoslav leadership and Stalin were deep-rooted. The revisionist views of the Yugoslav leadership were crystallized long before the liberation of their country, possibly since the time when the Communist Party of Yugoslavia was a member of the Comintern and worked in total illegality under the regime of the Serbian kings. Even at that time, its leadership had deviationist, Trotskyite views, which the Comintern condemned when they were expressed. Later Tito wiped off the condemnation by the Comintern, even going so far as to rehabilitate the greatest deviationist, the former general secretary of the Communist Party of Yugoslavia, Gorkic.

After the liberation of Yugoslavia a problem of great importance arose: what direction would Yugoslavia take? This direction, of course, would depend to a great extent on the Marxist-Leninist respectively revisionist world outlook of the leaders of the Communist Party of Yugoslavia. They passed themselves off as Marxist-Leninists. At first, we believed them. In fact, however, from their activity not only in general, but also from their concrete attitudes towards us, we observed many things about them which were not in conform with the scientific theory of Marxism-Leninism. We saw that they were moving away as far as possible from the experience of the construction of socialism in the Soviet Union.

It was the tendency of the Yugoslav leading group, headed by Tito, Kardelj, Rankovic and Djilas, a tendency which had been noticed since the time of their illegal activity but especially after the liberation of Yugoslavia, that the Communist Party of Yugoslavia should not come out openly under its own name, but should be disguised under the cloak of the so-called Popular

Front of Yugoslavia, as it was. This illegality was justified under the pretext that otherwise the big and petty bourgeoisie of the city and the countryside "could be worried and frightened off", that they "might abandon the new State power which had emerged from the revolution" and that "the Anglo-American allies might be frightened by communism". Efforts were made to convince the bourgeoisie that the communists were not in power, that the communist party existed but was, so to speak, a member in a broad front, in which Mihailovic's men, Nedic's men, Stojadinovic's men and the men of all the other reactionary "-vics" in Yugoslavia could participate.

Tito also formed a provisional government with Subasic, the former prime minister of the royal government in exile in London but under constant pressure from the people he did not permit it to govern very long and liquidated it. Then he pretended that he had not wanted Subasic but that the allies had imposed him, while later he accused Stalin of the same thing. The truth is that Tito accepted Subasic to please Churchill, that he did not like Stalin.

The views of Tito and his associates showed from the very beginning that they were far from being "hard-line Marxists", as the bourgeoisie calls the consistent Marxists, but "reasonable Marxists", who would collaborate closely with all the old and new bourgeois and reactionary politicians of Yugoslavia.

Although it claimed to be illegal, the Communist Party of Yugoslavia operated legally. Yet Rankovic and Tito did not give it the power and the leading role it should have had, because they were not for the construction of socialism in Yugoslavia. Tito and Rankovic distorted the Marxist-Leninist norms of the structure and the role of the party. The Communist Party of Yugoslavia was from the very beginning not built on the basis and the teachings of Marxism-Leninism. This party, which was allegedly merged with the Popular Front of Yugoslavia, made the law together with the Army, the Ministry of the Interior and the State Security service. This party which had led the war of the Yugoslav peoples became a detachment of the State organs of repression after the war - of the Army, the Ministry of the Interior and the UDB. Together with them, it also became an organ of oppression of the working masses, instead of being the vanguard of the working class.

The propaganda it used and the authority the party had won during the national liberation war and during the initial steps of the construction of Yugoslavia after the war gave the Yugoslavian working class the impression that this party was in the vanguard. In reality it was not the vanguard of the working class but of a new bourgeois class that had begun to settle in. This class relied strongly on the prestige of the national liberation war of the peoples of Yugoslavia for its own counter-revolutionary aims, while it obscured the perspectives of the construction of the new society. Such a degenerate party like this was bound to lead Titoite Yugoslavia on anti-Marxist paths.

The anti-Marxist course of the Yugoslav Titoites, of the Tito-Kardelj-Rankovic group, came – and this was inevitable - in open opposition to Marxism-Leninism, the communist parties, the Soviet Union, Stalin, and all the countries of people's democracy which were created after the Second World War. Of course, this clash developed gradually, till the critical moment came, when the chaff was separated from the wheat.

It is an undeniable fact that the peoples of Yugoslavia fought. Yugoslavia made great sacrifices, just as Albania did. The Yugoslavian anti-Marxist leaders abused this fight for their own goals, they also abused the Soviet appraisal of Yugoslavia for the public opinion at home and abroad, in which this country was described as an important ally on the Marxist-Leninist road to socialism.

It didn't take long till the Titoites displayed dominating tendencies, expansionism and hegemonism in their relations with the newly founded states of people's democracy, especially in their relations with our country. As we know they sought to

12

impose their anti-Marxist political, ideological, organisational and state views on us. They went so far as to make despicable attempts to transform Albania into a republic of Yugoslavia. In this unsuccessful and disgraceful undertaking the Titoites encountered our determined opposition. At first, our resistance was uncrystallised because we did not suspect that the Yugoslav leadership had set out on the capitalist and revisionist road. But after some years, when its hegemonic and expansionist tendencies were clearly displayed, we opposed them sternly and unreservedly.

The Titoites tried to impose their will on us by using the most various kinds of pressure and blackmail. To that end they also organized the conspiracy with Koci Xoxe. They pursued this same imperialist practice, although not to the same extent, towards other countries, too, like Bulgaria, Hungary, and Czechoslovakia. All these dirty acts clearly showed that Yugoslavia was not following the road to socialism, but had become a tool in the service of world capitalism.

With each passing day it was becoming clearer that a socialist society of the Leninist type was not being built in Yugoslavia, but that capitalism was developing instead. The steps taken on this capitalist road were meanwhile disguised with the alleged quest for new, specific forms of "socialism". Precisely for this purpose, the Yugoslav revisionist leadership with Tito, Kardelj, and Rankovic at the head, in an effort to somehow justify their betrayal "theoretically", borrowed the most various ideas from the arsenal of the old revisionists and in this way strengthened their fascist-type state by all possible means. The Army, the Ministry of the Interior, and the UDB became all-powerful.

Though it was establishing capitalism, the Yugoslav revisionist leadership tried to create the opinion among the masses of the people that the war aims were not being betrayed in Yugoslavia, that a state with a socialist orientation existed there, led by a communist party that defended Marxism and allegedly exactly because of this had come into opposition with the Soviet Union, Stalin, the communist parties and the countries of people's democracy.

To protect their positions which were badly shaken as a result of their exposure in front of the public opinion of the country and of the international communist and workers' movement, the Titoites, in continuation of their deceptive policy, proclaimed that they would take "serious" actions for the construction of socialism in the countryside, for the collectivization of agriculture according to Leninist principles and therefore they formed the so-called zadrugas. As for the seriousness of the intentions of the Titoite renegades about the construction of socialism in the countryside, it is enough to recall that the zadrugas collapsed before they were properly established and now no trace remains of the collectivisation of the Yugoslav countryside.

Up till 1948, when the final came split between the Soviet Union, the countries of people's democracy and the international communist movement on the one hand and Yugoslavia on the other, the latter was still in the initial phase of chaotic capitalism, in a state of political, ideological, economic disorganisation, in an extremely grave situation. This drove the Tito-Kardelj-Rankovic group to act more openly, to link itself more closely with world capitalism, especially US imperialism, in order to maintain its power and to change the situation to its advantage.

After 1948 Yugoslavia, being in a grave political, ideological and economic crisis, found itself at the crossroads because of the anti-Marxist deviation of its leadership. The Titoite renegades wanted, so to say, to sit on two "chairs". They wanted to sit on the chair of Marxism-Leninism merely for the sake of keeping up appearances, only for form's sake, while the wanted to plant themselves firmly on the other, the capitalist-revisionist "chair". But in order to achieve this aim, a certain amount of time would be necessary. The period from 1948 onwards was very troubled and shattered by the grave crises, by confusion and chaos.

The Tito-Kardelj-Rankovic group faced the question: How to keep power and crush any resistance by the proletariat and the peoples of Yugoslavia who had fought for socialism in friendship and complete unity with the Soviet Union and the countries of people's democracy? With this aim in view, the Yugoslav revisionists worked in the first place to liquidate any trace of Marxism-Leninism left in their party in order to transform it into an instrument of their bourgeois-revisionist ideology and policy, to divest it of any leading function. The working class was meant to be transformed into an inert mass which would not be able to see the betrayal and to fight against it as the decisive political force of the revolution. The norms of democratic centralism in the party were violated. The party was made dependent on the UDBA which was used as a mean to suppress all the elements who were not in favour of their regressive anti-Marxist turn. The party was "purged" of all those who were loyal to socialism. Though it appeared to retain some norms of elections, meetings and conferences, in reality its bureaucratic leadership concentrated all power in this allegedly Marxist-Leninist party in its own hands and transformed it into a mere tool for the implementation of its orders and those of the State Security Service. Thus the Communist Party of Yugoslavia was radically transformed and lost all the features of the vanguard party of the working class, the leading political force of society. This was a great victory for capitalism, for the foreign and local bourgeoisie.

In order to maintain their rule, the Titoite renegades had to quietly liquidate the state which had emerged from the national liberation war and to build another state, a ferocious fascist dictatorship.

In other words, the Tito-Kardelj-Rankovic leading group undertook the liquidation of all Marxist-Leninist features of the revolution and set out in quest of allegedly new "socialist" roads which were in fact capitalist in the economy, the internal and

15

foreign policy, education and culture and in all other sectors of life. In this situation the State Security organs and the Yugoslav Army became the favourite brutal weapon in the hands of this handful of renegades, who punished anybody in a draconian way who dared denounce the betrayal. The mass persecutions and killings of all sound Marxist-Leninist elements began. The dreadful concentration camps, one of which was that of Goli Otok, were filled with prisoners and internees.

At that time Yugoslavia's economy was in very bad situation. This was because of the war devastations, the confused policy of the Yugoslavian leadership and because of the breaking off of all relations with the Soviet Union, Yugoslavia no longer received the considerable aid it had received in the first years after liberation, as well as because it could no longer plunder the other countries of people's democracies, like Albania, through the "joint" companies set up on an unfair basis, which benefited only one side, namely Yugoslavia. Of course the Yugoslav renegades saw terror as the only way to get out of the crisis. As a long-standing agency of world capitalism, they immediately turned in that direction for aid and American imperialism in particular was ready to give Tito and co all the aid and support they needed to save their skins and to make them an important tool in its fight against socialism, the revolution and the liberation movements. The imperialist powers had been waiting impatiently for such a turn because they had been prepared for this since the time of the war. Therefore they did not fail to give them major economic "aid" but also gave them strong political-ideological support. They even supplied them with various weapons and military equipment and bound them to NATO by the Balkan Pact.

In the first period Yugoslavia was "aided" by capital investments from foreign companies, especially in industry and agriculture.

In the field of industry, where US imperialism showed itself particularly "generous", its "aid" enabled the beginning of the reconstruction of the old existing factories so that these could be made more or less operational and their production could suffice to keep the bourgeois-revisionist regime, which crystallized itself and which had turned its face towards world capitalism, on its feet.

The Titoite regime also had to liquidate that half-baked system of collectivization of agriculture which had been set up in a number of rural economies and to create a new system in which the kulaks and the great land owners would be favoured again. Forms and means were found for the redistribution of the land, under which the old kulaks were re-established without causing great unrests in the country. The state adopted a series of capitalist measures, such as the breaking up of the machine and tractor stations and the selling of their equipment to the rich peasantry which could afford to buy them as well as the imposition of heavy taxes on the peasants. The state farms, likewise, were transformed into capitalist enterprises in which also foreign capital was invested, etc.

The local merchants and industrialists, to whom major concessions were made, benefited greatly from the foreign capital invested.

These measures proved beyond any doubt that the "socialism" which was being built in Yugoslavia was nothing other than the road of integration into capitalism.

Thus the ground was prepared for the invasion of foreign capital on an ever larger scale, in a situation politically, ideologically and organisationally very suitable to world capitalism. The latter, by aiding the Titoite regime, would use it as a bridgehead for its push into the other countries of people's democracy.

This political, ideological and economic orientation of Titoite Yugoslavia towards capitalism made the class struggle there take another direction and did not develop any longer as a driving of the socialist society but as a driving power in the struggle among opposing classes, as is the case with any capitalist state where the dictatorship of the bourgeoisie prevails. The Titoite bourgeois-revisionist state spearheaded the class struggle in Yugoslavia against the progressive elements of the working class, against the communists who resisted the course of betrayal.

Democratic centralism was soon liquidated in the fields of the economic and state administration, too. It is true that in Yugoslavia some factories had been nationalized, the foreign trade had been proclaimed state monopoly and it was claimed that the principle of democratic centralism was implemented in the organization and activity of the state and the party. But these measures which seemed to have a revolutionary character were neither complete nor consistent. The centralism in Yugoslavia did not have the true Leninist meaning that the entire economic and political life of the society should be developed by combining the centralised leadership with the creative initiative of the local organs and the working masses. It rather aimed at creating a dictatorial force of the fascist type which would be in a position to impose the will of the regime in power on the peoples of Yugoslavia from above. As the years passed by these initial measures, which were advertised as allegedly socialist tendencies, took a clearly anti-Marxist, counter-revolutionary direction. The entire state organisation and State activity in the economic field adopted capitalist features in open opposition to the fundamental experience of the construction of socialism in the Soviet Union of Lenin and Stalin.

In the first years following 1948 we can say that the principle of centralism was implemented in the activity of the Yugoslav state, because the Federation of Yugoslavia had to carry very heavy and difficult burdens which it would not be able to solve decentralised. The times were such that the preservation of centralism was required because the Federation was made up of republics, each of them with different nationalist political currents, which were seeking to break away from it. But that sort of centralism was bureaucratic centralism, the economic plans

18

were decided from above without being discussed at the base, they were not well-studied and were not designed to promote an harmonious development of the various branches of the economy of the republics and regions of the Federation, the orders were arbitrary and were executed blindly, the products were procured by force. From this chaos, in which the initiative of the local organs of the party and state and the initiative of the working masses were nowhere to be seen, of course, disagreements were bound to emerge, as they did in fact, and they were suppressed by terror and bloodshed.

Such a situation was also encouraged by the capitalist states which had taken the Titoite regime under their wing in order to give Yugoslavia a capitalist orientation. Profiting from this state of affairs, the various imperialists were competing with each other in their efforts to get a tighter grip on this corrupt state so that, together with the credits they provided, they could also impose their political, ideological and organisational views.

The foreign capitalists who supported the Titoite renegade group recognised clearly that this group would serve them but they felt, after the turbulent and chaotic situation was overcome, that a more stable situation had to be created in Yugoslavia. Otherwise they could not be sure about the security of the big investments they were making and which they were to increase in the future.

In order to create the desired situation in favour of capitalism it was necessary to bring about the decentralisation of the management of the economy and the recognition and protection by law of the rights of the capitalists who were making large investments in the economy of this state.

The Tltoite leadership understood clearly that world capitalism wanted Yugoslavia, as a tool in its hands, to be in the best possible position to deceive others. Consequently it could not accept a bloodthirsty, openly fascist regime, which the anti-Marxists Tito-Kardelj-Rankovic had established. Because of this the group Tito-Kardelj took measures in 1967and liquidated the Rankovic group which was made responsible for all the evils of the Titoite rule up till that period.

With the liquidation of Rankovic, the League of "Communists" of Yugoslavia did not emerge from the crisis into which it had entered. It continued to be treated according to the old Titoite views, the essence of which was that the League should keep up only its "communist" disguise but never play the leading role in the state activity, the Army, or in the economy. The Titoites had even changed their party's name, calling it the "League of Communists", allegedly in order to give it an authentic "Marxist" name, taken from the dictionary of Karl Marx himself. The only officially recognised role of this so-called "League of Communists" was an educational one. But even this educational role was non-existent because Yugoslav society, which was lulled to sleep by the propaganda of an allegedly Marxist-Leninist policy and ideology, in the cradle of the so-called

"Socialist Alliance of Yugoslavia", was led astray on the capitalist road.

Although the Yugoslav revisionist party emerged from illegality it dissolved, as a result of the capitalist decentralisation, into that sort of ideological pluralism which later would be called "democratic" system. The main aim was that, after the party had been transformed into a bourgeois party, the capitalist features of the economic development of the country should be completely crystallised.

Thus suitable ground was prepared in Yugoslavia for the flourishing of anarcho-syndicalist theories, against which Marx, Engels, Lenin and Stalin had fought. Under these conditions the pseudo-Marxist-Leninist theory of the political system of "socialist self-administration", which Kardelj deals with in his book, was concocted.

I have dwelt a bit longer on the historical side of the

development of Yugoslavia on the revisionist road, not because these problems are unknown to us but in order to bring out more clearly the falsity of the "theoretical" ideas of Kardelj. As Tito's collaborator he cannot adopt any other position in the great betrayal of the revolution and socialism than that to presents white as black and to call capitalism socialism. Now, seeing the inglorious development to which they have brought their country, these renegades are trying to find "theoretical" justifications for the chaotic situation which they created themselves. This also explains Kardelj's obscure ideas. The Yugoslav reality is chaotic, too, and all the "theorising" about it is confusing. And how could it be any different?

2. The System of "Self-Administration" in the Economy

The theory and practice of Yugoslav "self-administration" is an outright denial of the teachings of Marxism-Leninism and the universal laws on the construction of socialism.

The essence of "self-administration socialism" in the economy is the idea that allegedly socialism cannot be built by concentrating the means of production in the hands of the socialist state by creating state ownership as the highest form of socialist ownership, but by fragmenting the socialist state property into property of individual groups of workers, who allegedly administer it directly themselves. Already in 1848 Marx and Engels stressed:

"The proletariat will use its political supremacy to wrest, by degrees, all capital from the bourgeoisie, to centralize all instruments of production in the hands of the State, i.e., of the proletariat organized as the ruling class" (K. Marx / F. Engels, Selected Works, vol. 1, p. 42 Tirana 1975, Alb. ed.)

Lenin stressed the same when he sternly combated the anarcho-syndicalist views of the group hostile to the party, the "Workers' Opposition", which demanded the handing of the factories to the workers and the management and organisation of production not by the socialist state but by a so-called "Congress of producers", as a representative of groups of individual workers. Lenin described these views as representing

"... a complete break with Marxism and communism" (V. I. Lenin, Collected Works, vol. 32, p. 283, Alb. ed.)

He pointed out that

"any justification, whether direct or Indirect, of the

ownership of the workers of a certain factory or a certain profession for their specific production, or any justification of their right to tone down or hinder the orders from general state power, is a gross distortion of the fundamental principles of Soviet power and complete renunciation of socialism" (V. I. Lenin, "On Democratisation and the Socialist Character of the Soviet Power")

In June 1950, when Tito presented the law on "self-administration" to the People's Assembly of the People's Federal Republic of Yugoslavia, while developing his revisionist views on ownership under "socialism", he said, among other things: "From now on state property in the means of production, factories, mines, railroads will gradually go over to the highest form of social ownership. State ownership is the lowest form of social ownership, not the highest form..." Among "the most characteristic acts of a socialist country" is "the transfer of factories and other economic enterprises from the hands of the state into the hands of the workers, for them to manage... " because in this manner the "slogan of the action of the working class - Factories to the Workers! - will be realized." ("Factories to the Workers", Prishtina 1951, pp. 37, 19, 1)

These assertions of Tito and the reactionary anarcho-syndicalist views of the "Workers' Opposition", which Lenin exposed in his time, are as like as two peas in a pot but they are also similar to the views of Proudhon, who wrote in his work "The Theory of Property" that "the spontaneous product of a collective unit... can be considered as the triumph of freedom... and as the greatest revolutionary force which exists and which can be opposed to the state." Or let us see what one of the leaders of the Second International, Otto Bauer, said in his book "The Road to Socialism": "Who, then, will lead socialised industry in the future? The government? No! If the government was to run all the branches of industry without exception, it would become too powerful over the people and the national representative body. Such an increase of government power would be dangerous for democracy" (Otto Bauer, "The road to Socialism", Paris 1919, p. 18)

In unity with Tito's views, E. Kardelj also stresses in his book: "Our society is compelled to act in this manner as soon as it has decided for self-government and the self-governing socialisation of the social property and against the perpetuation of the state-owned form of the socialist relations of production." (p. 66) [All quotations from E. Kardelj's book are taken from the Albanian translation by the Prishtina Publishing Board in 1977 - Publishing House "8 Nentori", Tirana]. This means that the system of private property has been established in Yugoslavia, and state socialist property, the property of the entire people, does not exist anymore.

Quite the opposite happens in our country, where this common socialist property is managed by the state of the dictatorship of the proletariat with the participation of the working class and the masses of working people in direct, centralised forms which are planned from below and orientated from above.

The course of the decentralisation of the means of production, according to the anarcho-syndicalist ideas of workers' "self-administration" is, in essence, nothing else but a clever way to preserve and consolidate capitalist private ownership over the means of production, although in a form disguised as "property administered by groups of workers". In fact, all the confusing and obscure terms invented by the "theoretician" Kardelj in his book, such as "fundamental organizations of united labour", "complex organisation of united labour", "workers' councils of the fundamental or complex organisations of united labour", "self-administrative communities of interests", etc. etc., which have even been written into the law of the Yugoslav capitalist state, are nothing but a glossy facade behind which the stripping of the working class of its right to ownership over the means of production, its savage exploitation by the bourgeoisie, is hidden.

This kind of private property exists in Yugoslavia not only in a disguised form but also in its open form, both in town and countryside. This, too, is admitted by E. Kardelj in his book when he says: "in our society such rights as... the right of personal property or, within given limits, also of private property... have special importance..." (p. 177). Kardelj tries in vain to play down the negative effect which the open acceptance of the right to private property might have even in the form of small-scale production, which, as Lenin says, gives birth to capitalism every day and every hour. The Yugoslav revisionists have issued special laws to encourage the private economy, laws which recognise the citizens' right to "found enterprises" and "to hire labour". The Yugoslav Constitution explicitly states: "Private owners have the same socio-economic position, the same rights and obligations as the working people in the socio-economic organisations."

Small private property reigns supreme in the Yugoslav agriculture and occupies nearly 90 per cent of the arable land. Nine million hectare of land belong to the private sector whereas over 10 per cent, or 1.15 million hectare belong to the monopoly, the so-called "social sector". Over 5 million peasants in Yugoslavia are engaged in cultivating privately-owned land. The Yugoslav countryside has never embarked on the road of genuine socialist transformations. Kardelj has not one word regarding this situation in his book and he avoids dealing with the problem how his system of "self-administration" is extended to agriculture. However, if he pretends that socialism is being built through this system, then how is it possible that he should have forgotten about "building socialism" in agriculture, too, which accounts for nearly half the economy? The Marxist-Leninist theory teaches us that socialism is built both in the city and in the countryside, not on the basis of state capitalist ownership, the ownership allegedly administered by workers' groups, or of private ownership in its open form, but only on the basis of socialist social ownership over the means of production.

In Yugoslavia private property of 10 to 25 hectare is

allowed (V. Vasic, "The Economic Policy of Yugoslavia", Prishtina University Press, 1970) But the Yugoslav law which permits the buying and selling, renting and mortgaging of land, the buying and selling of agricultural machinery and hired labour in agriculture has also created the possibilities for the new bourgeois class of the countryside, the kulaks, to add to the area of their land, means of work and implements, tractors and trucks at the expense of the poor peasants and consequently, to step up and intensify their capitalist exploitation.

Capitalist relations of production are so deeply rooted in the Yugoslav economy that even the capitalists from foreign companies have now a free field of action in making investments and, together with the local bourgeoisie, exploiting the local working class and the other masses of working people in Yugoslavia. The Yugoslav system of "self-administration" can rightly be described as a state of the co-operation of Yugoslav capitalism with US capitalism and other capitalists. They are partners sharing Yugoslavia's resources in all respects - in factories, means of communication, hotels, housing, up to the souls of people.

If the Yugoslav economy has made some steps forward in its development this is in no way due to the system of "self-administration", as the Titoite revisionists try to claim for themselves. Large amounts of capital from the capitalist world in the form of investments, credits and "aid" have been poured into Yugoslavia and this constitutes a considerable part of the material base of the Yugoslav capitalist-revisionist system. The debts alone amount over 11 billion dollars. Alone from the United States of America, Yugoslavia has received over 7 billion dollars in credits.

The international bourgeoisie did not support the Yugoslav system of "socialist self-administration" with such a material and financial base without a good reason. The crutches supplied by Western capital have kept this system on its feet as a model of the preservation of the capitalist order under pseudo-socialist labels.

With their investments, foreign capitalists have built numerous industrial projects in Yugoslavia which turn out products ranging from the highest to the lowest quality. Most of the best products are, of course, sold abroad and only a fraction of them are marketed within the country. Although there is great capitalist overproduction abroad and all the markets there are monopolised by the same capitalists who have invested in Yugoslavia they nevertheless sell the best Yugoslavian goods precisely on these markets for fabulous profits because labour power in Yugoslavia is cheap, products are turned out at a lower cost in comparison with the capitalist countries where the trade unions, more or less, make demands on capital in the workers' name. The best products the factories in Yugoslavia produce also go to he multinational companies which operate in Yugoslavia. However, on top of the profit they extract in this way, the foreign capitalist investors also squeeze out other profits - by the interest on the capital they have invested in Yugoslavia. These profits are often taken in the form of resources or raw material.

In his book, the demagogue Kardelj has a great deal to say about the system of "self-administration" but he maintains total silence about the presence and very major role of foreign capital in keeping the "self-administrative" system on its feet.

In the bourgeois countries, says Kardelj, the real power is based and "... manifested first of all in the relationships of the state executive power with the political cartels outside the parliament... parallel to the growth of the power of the extra-parliamentary internal force", Kardelj continues, "there is a new phenomenon, characteristic of contemporary social relations in the highly developed capitalist countries - the creation of the international or world-wide extra-parliamentary force." (p. 54). This way Kardelj seeks to prove that the Yugoslav "self-administration" has allegedly escaped such a situation. But as we explained in the foregoing the reality presents quite a different picture: the Yugoslav "self-administration" is a Yugoslav and

27

foreign capitalist joint administration. The foreign capitalists, that is, the companies, concerns and those who have made investments in Yugoslavia determine the policy and the all-round development of Yugoslavia just as much as the Yugoslav state power itself.

The so-called self-administrated enterprises, whether big or small, are in fact compelled to take account of the foreign investor. This investor has his own laws, which he has imposed on the Yugoslav State, has his own direct representatives in these joint companies and has his own representatives or his influence in the Federation. In fact, directly or indirectly, the investor imposes his will on the Federation, the joint enterprise or company. This is precisely what the "self-administration" is seeking to conceal. Kardelj needs this camouflage, this tour de passe-passe (conjuror's trick), as the French say, in order to "prove" the absurdity that Yugoslav "self-administration" is genuine socialism.

But what he endeavours to deny in his book is confirmed every day by many facts revealed by the Western press, indeed even by the Yugoslav news agency TANJUG itself which on the 16th of August that year reported about a new regulative issue of the "Federal Executive Veche" concerning the foreign investments in Yugoslavia. Under these regulations the rights of foreign capitalist investors in Yugoslavia are extended even further. "Under this law", reports TANJUG, "the foreign partners, on the basis of the agreements concluded between them and the organisations of socialised labour of this country, can make investments in currency, equipment, semi-finished and finished products and technology. Foreign investors have the same rights as the local organisations of socialised labour which invest their means in some other organisation of united labour."

Further on TANJUG stresses: "Under this set of regulations greater interest (on the part of foreigners) is anticipated, because it guarantees the security of the joint economic activity on a long-term basis. Besides this, there is now practically no field in which foreigners cannot invest their means, with the exception of social insurance, internal trade and social activities".

The country could not be sold to foreign capital more completely than this. And in face of this purely capitalist reality, the "communist" Kardelj still has the nerve to claim that "... our society has gained much strength in its socio-economic content and structure by the socialist and self-administrative relations of production..." which, he writes on, "... make possible and ensure that our society will develop more and more in a free, independent and self-governing manner..."! (pp. 7-8).

In Kardelj's book the individual is mainly considered as a chief element of society – the element which produces, the element which has the right to organise and to distribute production. According to him this element socialises work in an enterprise and exercises its leadership by the so-called workers' council which are "elected" by the workers and which allegedly regulates – together with the instituted administrative functionaries – the whole fate of the enterprise, the work, the income etc., within the system of "self-administration".

This is the typical form of capitalist enterprises where in fact it is the capitalist who rules, surrounded by a large number of officials and technicians who know the situation about the production and organise its distribution. Naturally, the bulk of the profits goes to the capitalist who owns the capitalist enterprise, that is, he appropriates the surplus value. Under the Yugoslav "self-administration" a large part of the surplus value is appropriated by the officials, the directors of the enterprises and the engineering technical staff. The "lion's share" goes to the Federation or the republic, in order to pay the fat salaries of the horde of officials of the central apparatus of the Federation or the republic. Funds are needed also to maintain the Titoite dictatorship - the Army, the Ministry of the Interior and the State Security Service, the Foreign Ministry etc., which are in the hands of the Federation and which are constantly inflated and extended. In this federal state a huge bureaucracy of non-producing officials and leaders, who are paid very high salaries from the sweat and blood of the workers and peasants, has developed. Apart from this a considerable part of the income is set aside for the foreign capitalist who has made investments in these enterprises and has his own representative in the "administrative council" or in the "workers' council", that is, he participates in the leadership of the enterprise. In this system labelled "self-administration socialism" the workers find themselves continuously under total exploitation.

The machinery of the "workers' councils" and "self-administration committees" with their commissions has been devised by the Belgrade revisionists simply to create the illusion among the workers that by being "elected" they take part and speak in these organs, it is allegedly them who decide the affairs of the enterprise, of "their" property. According to Kardelj, "... in the fundamental organisation of united labour... the workers run the activity of the organisation of united labour and the means of social reproduction... decide on all the forms of uniting and coordinating their own work and means as well as on all the income they make with their united labour... and divide the income for personal, joint, and general consumption in accord with the basis and criteria laid down on the basis of self-administration..." (p. 160) etc., etc.

All this is just nonsense because under the conditions that bourgeois democracy is ruling in Yugoslavia no genuine freedom of thought and action exists there for the workers. The freedom of action in the "self-administrated" enterprises is false. In Yugoslavia the worker does not run things, nor does he enjoy those rights which the "ideologist" Kardelj proclaims so pompously. In order to show that he is a realist and opposed to the injustices of his regime, Tito himself admitted recently in the speech he delivered at the meeting of leading activists of Slovenia that "self-administration" does not stop those who work badly from increasing their incomes at the expense of those who work well, while the directors of the factories who are to blame for the losses incurred can sneak out of their responsibility by taking responsible positions in other factories without worrying that somebody may reprimand them for the mistakes they committed.

Although E. Kardelj liquidated the bureaucracy and technocracy, eliminated the role of a dominant technocratic class "in theory", in reality, in practice this class was rapidly created and discovered a broad field of activity in this allegedly democratic system in which the role of the working man is supposedly "decisive". In fact, the role of that stratum of officials and the new bourgeoisie who dominate the "self-administrated" enterprise is decisive. It is them who draft the plan, who fix the amount of investments and everybody's income, the workers' and their own and, of course, they take good care of themselves first. Laws and rules were established in order to keep the profits of the leadership as high as possible and the wages of the workers low.

In Yugoslavia this narrow stratum of people, fattened on the workers' sweat and toil, who take decisions in their own interests, turned into a capitalist class. This is how the political monopoly in decision-making and division of income by the elite in the enterprises of socialist "self-administration" was created, while Kardelj continues to harp on the same old tune: that this political system, invented by the Titoites, contributes to the creation of conditions for the genuine realisation of the workers' "self-administration" and the "democratic" rights which the system recognises in principle.

The formation of the new capitalist class was encouraged precisely by the system of "self-administration". Tito himself has admitted this bitter fact as he allegedly made a "severe criticism" of the exploiters of workers, all those who run this system of "socialist self-administration" for their own profit. In many speeches, no matter how much he tried to hide the evils of his pseudo-socialist system, he had to admit the existence of the great crisis of this system and the polarisation of Yugoslav

31

society into rich and poor. "I do not consider the gains someone makes enrichment, even when he has been able to build a holiday cottage with his profits", says Tito. "But when it comes to a matter of hundreds of millions or even billions then this is theft... this is not wealth gained by one's own sweat... this wealth is being created through speculations of different kinds inside and outside the country... now we must look take a close look at those who are building houses - one in Zagreb, one in Belgrade and another at the seaside or some other place. And these are not simple holiday cottages but villas which can be rented out very well. Besides this, they have not just one but two or even three cars per family..." (Tito's interview with an editor of the newspaper "Vjesnik", October 1972). On another occasion, in order to show that he is against the stratification of society into rich and poor, Tito has also mentioned that some rich private persons have deposited about 4.5 billion dollars in the Yugoslav banks alone without taking account of how much they have deposited in foreign banks and how much they carry in their pockets.

In writing about the system fabricated by the Titoite revisionists, Kardelj is compelled to shortly mention the need for the fight "... against the various forms of distortions and attempts to usurp the rights of self-government of the workers and citizens." (p. 174). But again he seeks the way out of these "misuses" within the system of "self-administration" by "... extending the respective mechanism of democratic social control..." (p. 178).

Here the question arises: to what class is Kardelj referring when he speaks about the "usurpation of the workers' right to self-government"? Of course, though he does not say so, here he is referring to the old and new bourgeois class which has usurped the power of the working class and is riding on its back and exploiting it to the bone.

Kardelj tries in vain to present "the workers' councils", "the fundamental organizations of united labour", etc. etc., as the most authentic expression of "democracy" and the "freedom" of man in all social fields. The "workers' councils" are nothing but entirely formal organs, defenders and implementers not of workers' interests but of the will of the directors of enterprises because, being materially, politically and ideologically corrupted, these councils have become part of the "worker aristocracy" and "worker bureaucracy", agencies to mislead and to create false illusions among the working class.

Yugoslav reality shoes clearly that there is no genuine democracy for the masses there. And it cannot be otherwise. Lenin stressed that

"'industrial democracy' is a term that lends itself to misinterpretations. It may be read as a repudiation of dictatorship and individual authority. It may be read as a suspension of ordinary democracy or as a means of evading it." (V. I. Lenin, Collected Works, Vol. 32, p. 80, Alb. ed.)

There cannot be a socialist democracy for the working class without its state of dictatorship of the proletariat. Marxism-Leninism teaches us that negation of the state of the dictatorship of the proletariat is a negation of democracy for the masses of working people.

The negation of the state of the dictatorship of the proletariat and the socialist social property on which it is based, by the Yugoslav revisionists, has led them to a decentralised management of the economy without a unified state plan. The development of the national economy on the basis of a unified state plan and its management by the socialist state on the basis of the principle of democratic centralism is one of the universal laws and fundamental principles of the construction of socialism in every country. Otherwise capitalism is built, as in Yugoslavia.

Kardelj claims that the workers in their "self-administrative" organizations have the right "... to govern the work and the activity of the organisation of united labour..." (p. 160), i.e., of the enterprises, hence they can also allegedly plan production. But what is the truth? In these organisations the worker neither runs nor constructs so-called basic plan. The new bourgeoisie does these things, the leadership of the enterprise, while the workers are given the impression that the "workers' councils" supposedly make the law in this "self-administrative" organisation. This happens in the capitalist countries, too, where the power of the private enterprise is in the hands of the capitalist who has his own technocracy, his technocrats who run the enterprise, while in some countries there are also the workers' representatives with a negligible function, just enough to create the illusion among the workers that they, too, allegedly take part in running the affairs of the enterprises But this is a lie.

The so-called planning which is done in the Yugoslavian "self-administrative" enterprises cannot be called socialist but, on the contrary, is carried out according to the example of all capitalist enterprises - it leads to the same consequences which exist in every capitalist economy, such as anarchy of production, spontaneity and a series of other contradictions which manifest themselves in the most overt and savage manner in the Yugoslav economy and market.

Kardelj writes that

"... the free exchange of labour through the production of commodities and the free, self- governed market (emphasis ours) at the present level of the socio-economic development is a condition for self-government... This market... is free in the sense that the self-governing organisations of united labour freely and with the minimum of administrative intervention, enter into relations of the free exchange of labour. The suspension of such freedom is bound to lead to the regeneration of the state property monopoly of the state apparatus." (p. 95).

There could be no more flagrant denial than this of the teachings of Lenin, who wrote:

We must foster 'proper' trade, which is one that does not evade state control, it is beneficial to support it ...for the free

34

market is a development of capitalism..." (V. I. Lenin, Collected Works, Vol. 32, pp. 426, 213, Alb. ed. - emphasis ours).

From the political economy of socialism it is known that, under socialism, trade, like all other processes of social reproduction, is a process which is planned and directed in a centralised manner, which is based on the socialist social ownership of the means of production and itself is a constituent part of the socialist relations of production. However, these teachings are totally alien to the revisionist Kardelj and this results in his denial of the economic role of the socialist state and socialist property. The Yugoslav home market is a typical decentralised capitalist market where the means of production are freely sold and purchased by anyone, which is contrary to the laws of socialism. For these reasons TANJUG is forced to admit that entrepreneurs, middlemen and speculators dominate all Yugoslav trade. Chaos, spontaneity, catastrophic fluctuations of prices, etc. prevail in the market. According to data from the Yugoslav Federal Institute of Statistics, prices for 45 main products and social services increased 149.7 per cent in the period from 1972 to 1977 in Yugoslavia.

In regard to sales of commodities inside the country purchasing power is very weak in Yugoslavia because of the low wages of the workers and also because, in the final balance of enterprises, there is not much left to be distributed among the workers. The enterprise wants to sell its products anywhere it can and in an independent manner, because the principal leaders, that is, the bosses, the new bourgeoisie, want to create profits. But where can they create the profits they want when the purchaser is poor? Therefore they have contrived new forms, one of which is the sale of goods on time payment. The selling of goods turned out in these "self-administrated" enterprises on time payment is another chain around the necks of the Yugoslav workers, just as the workers of the capitalist countries are chained by the same capitalist system which, is called "socialist self-administration" in Yugoslavia.

Similar features also characterise Yugoslav foreign trade in which no state monopoly exists. Depending on the wishes of its owners every enterprise can conclude contracts and agreements with any firm, multinational company or foreign state to buy or sell raw materials and machinery, finished products, technological means, etc. This anti-Marxist policy also has had its influence on the Yugoslav State becoming a vassal of world capital and on its deep involvement in the economic and financial crisis which holds the entire capitalist-revisionist world in its grip, a crisis which is also manifested in other fields.

As a die-hard revisionist, E. Kardelj also denies the role of the socialist state in other fields, such as financial relations and other activities of various character. He writes that " the relations in the fields on which the self-governing communities of interest are founded, are realised according to regulations without the intervention of the state, that is, ...without the intermediary of the budget and other administrative-fiscal measures... (p.167).

In Yugoslavia, just as in the other capitalist countries, the system of the provision of credits by the banks instead of the budgetary financing of investments for the development of the productive forces and other activities, has become very popular. The banks have become centres of financial capital and it is precisely them that play a very important role in the Yugoslav economy - in the interests of the new revisionist bourgeoisie.

Thus an anarcho-syndicalist system has been established in Yugoslavia and this has been named "socialist self-administration". What has this "socialist self-administration" brought to Yugoslavia? All kinds of evil. Anarchy in production in the first place. Nothing is stable there. Each enterprise throws its products on the market and capitalist competition takes place because there is no coordination, since it is not the socialist economy which guides production. Each enterprise goes it alone, competing against the other, in order to ensure raw materials, markets and everything else. Many enterprises are closing down because of lack of raw materials, the huge deficits created by this chaotic capitalist development, the build-up of stocks of unsold goods due to the lack of purchasing power and the saturation of the market with outdated goods. Yugoslavia's handicrafts services are in a very serious state, too. Referring to this problem at the meeting of Slovenia's leading activists, Tito could not hide the fact that "Today you have to sweat a good deal to find, for example, a carpenter or some other craftsman to repair something for you and even when you find him you are fleeced so blatantly that it makes your hair stand on end."

Regardless of the previously mentioned fact that some of the modern combines turn out good quality products, a difficult situation is created for Yugoslavia because it has to find a market for the sale of these commodities. Because of these difficulties Yugoslavia's balance of foreign trade is passive. Just in the first 5 months of this year the deficit was 2 billion dollars. At the 11th Congress of the League of "Communists" of Yugoslavia, Tito declared that "the deficit with the Western market has become almost intolerable". Nearly three months after this congress, he declared again in Slovenia: "We have especially great difficulties in trade exchanges with the European Common Market member countries. There the imbalance constantly very seriously about this. Many of them promise us that these things will be put in order, that imports from Yugoslavia will increase, but up to now we have had very little benefit from all this. Each is putting the blame on the other." And the deficit in foreign trade, which Tito does not mention in this speech of his, exceeded 4 billion dollars in 1977. This is a catastrophe for Yugoslavia. The entire country is in the grip of an unending crisis, and the broad working masses live in poverty.

Many Yugoslavian workers are out of work, are being thrown into the street or emigrating abroad. Tito has not only acknowledged this economic emigration, this capitalist phenomenon, but has even recommended that is should be encouraged. Unemployment cannot exist in a socialist country, the best example for this is Albania. Meanwhile in the capitalist countries, among which Yugoslavia is of course included, unemployment exists and is developing everywhere. When Yugoslavia has over one million unemployed, and over 1.3 million economic emigrants are selling their labour power in West Germany, Belgium, France, etc., when the wealth of individuals occupying important posts either in the state administration or in enterprises and institutions is increasing rapidly, when the prices of consumer goods are mounting day by day, when the bankrupt enterprises and branches number thousands, the system of Yugoslav "self-administration" is proved to be a great fraud. And yet Kardelj, without being ashamed in the least, has the temerity to write: "In our conditions, socialist self-administration is the most direct form and expression of the struggle for the freedom of the working man, for the freedom of his labour and creativity, for his decisive economic and political influence in society." (p. 158).

Deepening his bourgeois type of demagogy by stale phrases, Kardelj reaches a new level of deception, saying: "With the constitutional and legal guarantee of the workers' rights on the basis of their socialised labour in the past, our society further extends the dimensions of real freedom for the workers and working people in the material relations of society." (p. 162). And what does this apologist of the bourgeoisie have in mind when he talks of the extension of the "dimensions of true freedom for the workers"? Is it the "freedom" to be unemployed, the "freedom" to leave their families and homeland in order to sell the power of own muscles and minds to the capitalists of the Western world or is it the "freedom" to pay taxes, to be discriminated against and savagely exploited by the old and the new Yugoslav bourgeoisie as well as by the foreign bourgeoisie?

3. "Self administration" and the Anarchist Views on the State.

The National Question in Yugoslavia

In Yugoslavia organs of State power as genuine representatives of the people do not exist. There only exists the bureaucratic system called "the system of delegates", which is presented as the alleged bearer of the system of state power, and that is why no elections for deputies to the organs of State power are held. The Titoites want to justify this fact by arguing that the representative organs are allegedly expressions of bourgeois parliamentarism and of the Soviet socialist State which, according to them, Stalin had allegedly turned into an institution of bureaucracy and technocracy. The experience of the Soviets of the worker and peasant deputies, set up by Lenin based on the immense experience of the Paris Commune was disregarded, the Yugoslavian revisionists labelled it "forms of state organising which create personal power".

Developing the revisionist idea of "specific socialism", the Titoites sometime in the fifties declared in the face of the whole world that they would ultimately renounce the socialist state system and had replaced it with a new system, the system of "self-administrative socialism", in which socialism and the state are alien for each other. This revisionist "discovery" was nothing less than a copy of Proudhon's and Bakunin's anarchist theories about the "workers self-management" and the "workers' factories", which have long been exposed as crude corruption of of Marx and Lenin's true ideas about the state and the dictatorship of the proletariat.

Karl Marx writes:

Between capitalist and communist society lies the period

of the revolutionary transformation of the one into the other. Corresponding to this is also a political transition period in which the state can be nothing but the revolutionary dictatorship of the proletariat.

The political system of "socialist self-administration" has not only nothing in common with the dictatorship of the proletariat but is even opposed to it. This system is constructed after the model of the administration of the united States of America. Kardelj himself wrote about the Yugoslav "system of self-administration": ... we could say that this system is more similar to the organisation of the executive power in the United States of American than in Western Europe..." (p. 235)

From this follows clearly that the fact, that the organisation of the Yugoslav government is a copy of the organisation of capitalist governments, is not denied but what could be discussed is the question: which capitalist government has been imitated the most, the American or one of the Western European governments. And for this discussion Kardelj provides the solution when he says: the organisation of the executive power of the United States of America has been chosen as model.

The Yugoslav revisionists' views about the state are trough and through anarchist. As is well-known anarchism demands the immediate elimination of every form of state, so of the dictatorship of the proletariat, too. And the Yugoslavian revisionists have eliminated the dictatorship of the proletariat and in order to justify this betrayal the speak of two different phases of socialism – "state socialism" and the "true humanitarian socialism". According to their opinion the first phase contains the first years after the victory of the revolution, in which the dictatorship of the proletariat exists, which expresses itself in the "etatist-bureaucratic" state, just like in capitalism. The second phase is the phase of the overcoming of the "etatist-bureaucratic state" and its replacement trough "direct democracy". With those views the Titoites not only deny the necessity of the dictatorship of the proletariat in socialism, but also contrast the terms socialist state, dictatorship of the proletariat and socialist democracy with each other.

They pay no attention to the classics of Marxism-Leninism which teach that the socialist state is continuously consolidated during the whole historical period of transition from capitalism to communism. Therefore E. Kardelj writes that society in Yugoslavia is less and less based on the role of the state apparatus. According to him the state in Yugoslavia is allegedly withering away.

But with what does Kardelj replace the role of the state apparatus? He replaces it by the "initiative of the workers"! He expresses it this way: "... the further functioning of our society will be based less and less on the role of the state apparatus and more and more on the power and initiative of the workers..." (p.8) An absurd judgement! To speak of the initiative of the workers means that the workers above all have to be free and organised, inspired by clear directives, have to take measures to implement those initiatives. Who concerns themselves in Yugoslavia with organising and inspiring the workers through clear directions? The "self-administrated community", says Kardelj in his abstract judgement. He leaves the leading part in this sort of community to the individual "in the united self-administrated work of his interests". What is meant by this "self-administrated unity" of the individual's interests, which stands in the centre of Yugoslav society, is nowhere clearly explained. But what emerges of this idea is bourgeois individualism which puts the absolute rights of the individual in society and its complete independence of this society, the priority of personal interests over the interests of society first.

According to this "theoretician", who permits himself to such judgement the consolidation of the state and its apparatus is characteristic for the forms of "government property of the socialist relations of productions..." (p.8). In Yugoslavia in contrast, he says, the process of consolidation of the "self-administrative" role of the working class will develop in contrast

41

to the state. According to this "philosopher" man cannot be free and master of his fate in a genuine socialist state where Marxist-Leninist science and the Leninist revolutionary practice are applied, but is transformed into a machine. In Yugoslav "self-administration", in contrast, the worker allegedly assumes great importance and precisely in this "self-administration", in the "democratic mechanism of delegation of Yugoslav society", he understands his great role! Which classes do these state organs represent, which ideology guides them, on what principles have they built their activity and to what forum do they render account? Of course no clear answer to these all these questions can be found because any accurate answer would shed light on Yugoslavia's capitalist political system.

Kardeij sticks to his anarchist positions when he writes, making no distinction at all about what state, party or system he is referring to, attacking the State in general for being inhuman: "Neither the state, nor the system, nor the political party can bring happiness to man. Man alone can bring happiness to himself" (p. 8).

Here the tendencies for spontaneity in the anti-Marxist theory of "socialist self-administration" are brought to surface quite clearly, according to which the working class needs not organise itself in the party or the State to achieve its aspirations but will find the happiness it looks for even while wandering in the dark as time goes by.

To anticipate the question: "If the state is unnecessary why is it not eliminated in Yugoslavia then?" Kardelj wrote: "The State... must interpose in the role of the arbiter only in those situations when the self-governing agreement cannot be achieved but it is essential from the aspect of social interests that a decision is made" (p. 23). And to prove that allegedly the need for state arbitration to settle disagreements is rare, Kardelj says: "The free exchange of labour has an essential influence on reducing the antagonisms between physical and mental work. In this relations mental work is no longer superior to physical work but is only

42

one of the components of the free united labour and of the free exchange of different forms of the results of labour" (p. 24). Upon reading these phrases, the question arises in everybody's mind: is it possible that the author talks about the Yugoslav social order here? Since when have the antagonisms between mental and physical work been reduced in Yugoslavia?!

The reality of development in Yugoslavia proves the opposite. There are essential distinctions between mental and physical work which cannot be reduced by words. It is really astonishing that there is talk about the reduction of antagonisms between mental and physical work in the Yugoslav state, it is known that alone the wage differentials between a worker and an intellectual there, not to speak about other distinctions - have reached a ratio of one to twenty, if not more.

Kardelj considers "self-administration in the united work" as "...the genuine material basis for self-administration in society, too, that is to say, in the socio-political communities which exercise state power from the commune up to the federation, as well as for the realisation of the democratic rights of working people and citizens in the running of the state, or respectively, of society. Self-government is also the material basis for the development of the worker as a creative individual in the utilization of all sorts of social means..." (p. 24) and many other such phrases.

Seeking to present the so-called self-administration as the material premise for man's happiness, which the great minds of Yugoslavia have allegedly "discovered" for us, Kardelj resorts to twisted phrases and ecclesiastical language, preaching a long sermon but essentially saying nothing. He lines up contradictory ideas about "scientific socialism" and uses lengthy expressions in order to give his words an alleged profound philosophical meaning.

But how is the Yugoslav political system carried out in practice? When it comes to answering this question, Kardelj is forced to admit: "In this respect there are excessive weak points in the system. A whole series of weaknesses in the functioning of the organizations and institutions of our political system rightfully gives the impression that powerful sources of bureaucracy and technocracy are still operating, that our administration is complicated and that it is therefore is overgrown with bureaucracy, that some organs and organizations are secluding themselves, that there are many gaps and cases of duplication of work, that the forms of democratic communication between self-governed and state organs and the entire social structure are weakly developed, that we hold many useless and fruitless meetings, that the meetings and decisions are frequently insufficiently prepared from the professional viewpoint, that in the fight for his rights the citizen often has difficulties to overcome the administrative obstacles etc." (p. 193). So if the system of "self-administration" chokes on bureaucracy, if the state and administrative organs are secluded, make worthless decisions and shut out the citizens who want them to do something about their many troubles - then who, apart from the Tito clique, needs this system? How can the Yugoslav citizens govern themselves when they cannot overcome the "administrative obstacles"? Despite all the great efforts of the devil not to show his cloven foot, despite all the reservations and efforts to round things off by the Titoite ideologist in order to cover up the dark sides of his system – even what he admits is enough to realize the truth.

Kardelj writes: "Both the structure of delegates' assemblies and the way decisions are taken there are organized in such a way that they in principle ensure the leading role of the united labour in the whole system of making state decisions" (pp. 24-25). With these words he is trying to create a focus to show that the "delegates' assemblies", which in reality are very similar to the assemblies set up by capitalist trade unions, where the trade union members indulge in idle talk, can allegedly exercise state functions. Therefore, according to him, the state of the

44

dictatorship of the proletariat is superfluous.

Here, of course, it is not a matter of replacing the name of the dictatorship of the proletariat, which terrifies the bourgeoisie and the revisionists, with another name: "delegates' assemblies". No, this here is about changing the class character of the socialist state, so that not the working class but the new bourgeoisie holds power. It is not difficult to see that these positions aim at justifying the course of returning to capitalism and, as far as possible, the Titoite betrayal.

In order to present their notorious system of "socialist self-administration" as correct and acceptable, the Titoites oppose it to the dictatorship of the bourgeoisie and the dictatorship of the proletariat. For the Titoites all other political systems, without making distinction between capitalism and socialism, are "dogmatic". First they call their phantasms "system of socialist self-administration", then, in order to demonstrate the superiority of their system, they compare it with the capitalist social order.

Of course the Yugoslav revisionists cannot fail to "find fault" with the parliamentary political system of bourgeois society, which Kardelj defines as a "multi-party system", for otherwise they would expose themselves as advocates of bourgeois parliamentarianism, which Marx and Lenin sternly criticised in their time. Therefore they declare that it would be a mistake to consider this political form of the bourgeois state as having a universal and eternal character. The whole world knows that Kardelj was not the first to "criticize" the bourgeois ideologists' notorious thesis about the universal and eternal character of capitalism. In refuting the views of social-democracy the classics of Marxism-Leninism proved scientifically that the capitalist system is by no means universal and eternal, that it is doomed to die, that the capitalist state, which is the offspring and bulwark of this system hostile to the people, must be destroyed to its foundations and in its place the true socialist system must be established, but not a bastardized system which starts from capitalism and returns again to capitalism, as the Yugoslav

45

political system of "self-administration" does.

Kardelj "criticizes" the bourgeois parliamentary system, but lightly and gently, because it hurts him to do so and therefore, immediately after criticizing it, he praises its contribution to the democratic development of mankind to the skies and makes a fetish of it. In order to exaggerate this contribution in such a way that the reaction character of today's bourgeois parliament pales into insignificance and in particular to show the "organic link between parliamentarianism and democratic human rights", for the first time he quotes (or rather mutilates) Marx: "The parliamentary regime lives on debate, then how can it ban discussion? Every social interest and institution is transformed into general ideas here, is treated as idea so how is it possible then for any interest or institution to stand above all ideas and impose itself like a religious dogma?... A parliamentary regime allows the majority to decide everything, how is it possible then that the overwhelming majority outside parliament does not want to take decisions?"

This quotation from Marx is like a square peg in a round hole in the context of this book, therefore it can hardly serve to prove what Kardelj wants. Marx's idea, in the tricky way it was quoted by this revisionist, out of context and mutilated, casts doubt on the undeniable fact that Marx was absolutely opposed to the venal and rotten bourgeois parliamentarianism.

This attempt on the author's part is unsuccessful because everybody knows Marx's stance who, when criticizing the bourgeois parliament and the bourgeois theory of the division of powers, never said that representative institutions should be done away with and that the principle of elections should be abandoned, as it was done in Yugoslavia. In fact he wrote that in the proletarian state such representative organs should be set up and operate that are not "talking shops" but real working institutions, built and acting as

"...a working body, executive and legislative at the same

time." (K. Marx / F. Engels, Selected works,,vol. 2, p. 544, Tirana 1975, Alb. ed.)

Bourgeois parliamentarianism has gained "great strength" because, as the author of the book claims, socialist practice, with the exception of Yugoslavia, has been unable to develop new forms of democratic life corresponding to socialist relations of production more rapidly and extensively. The new form of democratic life, according to Kardelj, has allegedly been realised under "socialist self-administration" which crossed the Rubicon of class state power of the owners and of the technocratic-monopolistic managers of capital. One can only be amazed at him describing all the efforts of the democratic forces to find forms of democracy as "artificial constructions" of the bourgeois Parliament, as attempts to unite "several things that cannot be united", whereas he calls the constructions of Yugoslavia's "socialist self-administration", these bastardized grafts of the bourgeois-revisionist forms of government, original and socialist! If there ever was fraud in the construction of governing it is to be found in the first place in the anti-Marxist and anti-democratic theories of the Titoites' self-administration Regardless of the numerous deceptive statements made about it, Yugoslav "self-administration" is a copy of bourgeois parliamentarianism and of capitalist relations of production; it is a chaotic appendage of the world capitalist system, of the structure and superstructure of this system.

"Our socialist democracy", writes Kardelj, "would not be an all-embracing system of democratic relations without the relevant solution of the problems of relations among Yugoslavia's nations and nationalities" (p. 171). Although the revisionist ideologist would have had to explain at this occasion how the political system of "socialist self-administration" has solved the problem of nations and nationalities in Yugoslavia, he forwent so widely around this major problem, so serious and delicate for his federation, that after reading his book of 323 pages one can barely recall that there was any talk about nations and nationalities.

How about the problem of nations and nationalities in Yugoslavia? The Yugoslav Federation inherited deep-rooted conflicts in this field. The policies of the Great-Serbian Kings and reactionary chauvinistic circles in Yugoslavia was such that, it historically stirred up conflicts and hostility among nations and nationalities.

After Second World War, the Federal Republic of Yugoslavia launched the slogan "unity - fraternity" but this slogan proved quite inadequate to solve the differences inherited from the past, therefore the old conflicts, the unrestrained craving for domination over others did not disappear. Tito and the renegade clique around him did not carry out a Marxist-Leninist national policy in regard to the tendencies of republics and regions to break away from the Federation. On the contrary, the relations among nationalities remained the same as in the time of the Kings and in regard to some nationalities the genocide went on as before. This policy served to fuel the hatred and quarrels among the nations and nationalities of Yugoslavia. The "unity" and "fraternity" of peoples about which there is a great deal of talk in Yugoslavia, has never been presented on the correct basis of the economic, political, social and cultural equality of nations and nationalities.

Without achieving equality in these fields the national question in Yugoslavia cannot be solved correctly. For three decades now "self-administrative socialism" has, apart from its demagogy about the" self-governing community of nations and nationalities of a new type", done nothing about the implementation of the sovereign rights of these different nations and nationalities in the republics and regions of Yugoslavia. The Kosova region, for example, with an Albanian population almost three times bigger than the population of the Republic of Montenegro, has a distinct economic, political, social and cultural backwardness in comparison with the other regions of Yugoslavia. In the larger Republics, too, impermissible distinctions exist in all fields compared with the other Republics. This situation is the weakest spot which is shaking the Federation of the Yugoslav revisionists to its foundations. Pious hopes about a solution to the old and new differences among Yugoslavia's nations are futile.

From an objective and scientific analysis of this very difficult and troubled situation, the incontestable conclusion emerges that the national question in Yugoslavia will not be solved unless Marxism-Leninism is implemented there, unless the capitalist so-called self-administrative order is overthrown.

The Titoite renegades feel this danger and therefore, if they have to mention the problems of nations and nationalities, they try to bridge the gap with pompous statements without getting to the crux of the problems, or by seeking false testimony from other revisionists, as they did when they gave great publicity to the declarations of the Chinese revisionists about the Marxist-Leninist solution of the national problem in Yugoslavia.

In words the revisionists may present the relations among the nations and nationalities of Yugoslavia as they like, but the bitter truth of this problem will still haunt them beyond death.

The national question in Yugoslavia will be solved by the peoples of the present Federation themselves and not by those who, regardless of what they say, in fact are still pursuing the reactionary and chauvinistic policy of their predecessors.

Continuing his explanations about the policy of the Yugoslav state, the cunning revisionist Kardelj claims that this policy is "... no longer the monopoly of professional politicians and political cartels behind the scenes" but instead it becomes "a matter of direct activity and of direct decision-making by the self-governors and their organs..." (p. 25). Behold, Kardelj wants to say, henceforth do not criticise us for betraying the interests of the working class anymore because the Yugoslav worker is master of the policy of the country and of the defense of his "self-administrative" interests, unlike in the other States where professional politicians are the masters. And here, too, in bad faith he makes no difference between capitalist and socialist countries but lumps them all together because in this manner it is easier to present black as white.

Kardelj knows that in order to realise the dishonest aims he has in mind he has to trivialise the manifestations which expose the "self-administrative" reality in every way. Therefore he belittles the fact that the Yugoslav worker has no chances of realising his rights in the political and economic field and explains that this "is due to a series of objective and subjective reasons – among which, undoubtedly, the still relatively low level of education and culture and the level of the application of science belongs - the worker is not yet able to dominate, orientate, or completely control in a conscious and creative manner all the processes which the his social and economic position imposes on him." (p. 27). It is obvious that this was written in order to defend anti-worker and anti-socialist positions. At present the Yugoslav worker understands nothing of this illusory theory and he also does not see any of these false and absurd ideas, which are unacceptable to him, being implemented in practice.

Since the low cultural and scientific level of the workers is an obstacle, as Kardelj says, the main role in the "self-administrative" society is played by the educated and skilled people, who are the ruling elite in this "socialist community". Under these circumstances decisions will be taken in most instances precisely by this elite, by the cultured element of the new bourgeoisie which makes the law in Yugoslavia. Who is to blame that the elite is becoming prominent and the role of the workers is diminishing? There is no doubt the blame lies within the very social system which generates the new capitalist class and provides it with the possibilities to strengthen itself economically at the expense of the workers and become educated, while the working class is left at a low level. Kardelj cannot avoid to mention the fact that in practice decisions are taken by a relatively small percentage of people in Yugoslavia. However, he has nothing to say about the fact that this is precisely the way how the political monopoly of the elite in taking decisions and in the division of the income in the enterprises of "socialist self-administration" is created. This political monopoly, which the Yugoslav revisionists allegedly guard themselves against and combat, is particularly striking in their so-called political system of "socialist self-administration".

In the "self-administrated" society, as Kardelj expresses it "...instead of the old relationships: the worker - the state - social activities, a new relationship must inevitably be constituted between the workers engaged directly in production and the workers in social activities." (p. 23). According to him, building social relations by the way of a socialist regime where scientific socialism is applied, where there is unity between the workers directly involved in production and the workers engaged in social activities, where there is vigorous socio-political activity and an organization of the economy in which the principal role is played by the working people organized in their socialist state is not the correct way. The correct way, according to Kardelj, is that of building "new" social relations without the participation of the state!

These ideas are an expression of pure anarchism. All these phrases are are only there to obscure anything good a genuine socialist regime offers and to treacherously claim that in Yugoslavia they are allegedly marching towards the unity of the workers and intellectuals through the "free exchange of labour", which reduces their antagonism as if by magic.

In Kardelj's theory there is not any mention of the violent overthrow of the capitalist state, of the seizure of power by the working class and the establishment of the dictatorship of the proletariat, nor can there be. Although he quotes Marx's words that "at given moments we have to resort to violence which will finally constitute the power of labour" he does this only to prove that Marx allegedly leaned more towards the triumph of the

51

proletarian revolution by peaceful means, while considering violence an exception and making it conditional on some particular social circumstances. And with such sophistry Kardelj seeks to create the impression that the working class nowadays can achieve its historical interests not through revolution, but in alliance with the various political parties of the capitalist countries. Kardelj has copied this cunningly way of quotation to pit Marx against Marx in regard to the possibility of the peaceful transition to socialism from his revisionist predecessors, against whom Lenin wrote:

"The reference to what Marx... said about the possibility of peaceful transition to socialism... is the argument of a sophist, which means in ordinary words, of an imposter, who is juggling with quotations and references for his trickery." (V. I. Lenin, Collected Works, Vol. 28, p. 107, Alb. ea.)

Kardelj needs these falsifications in order to lend a hand to the "Eurocommunists", with whom he is in complete accord. The revisionist parties of Italy, France and Spain have declared that they will allegedly achieve socialism through the development of bourgeois democracy and freedoms, through the force of the ballot in parliamentary elections. According to the "Eurocommunists" the ability of the working class will be expressed in the question to what extent it it will gain the key positions in the structure of capitalist society and the state, as well as in the running of society. This way, they say, the transformation of the character of the capitalist relations of production to "self-administrative" or "socialist" relations of production will become possible. It is precisely on this issue that the Titoite theory and the theory of "Eurocommunism" are united. The "Eurocommunists" are obliged to accept European bourgeois political pluralism and the unity among bourgeois parties in order to - allegedly through reforms - be able to ensure many rights for working class and then, enable the transformation to "socialist" society on this way. Kardelj calls these efforts of his friends "structural changes", which must exert without doubt such an influence that the process develops and thereby transforms both the position and role of the parliament itself.

Therefore Kardelj's theory claims that the "communist" parties of Western Europe under the conditions of the crisis of the capitalist system, while preserving the parliamentary system whose democratic achievements – as he says - cannot be denied, must find an appropriate way to secure an alliance with the broadest "democratic" forces for the working class. Through this sort of alliance, according to revisionist logic, a more favourable "democratic" situation can be created in the parliamentary system and in the long run the parliamentary system – who knows how - will be "transformed" into a decisive power of the people! This is the course Titoism sets for the other revisionist parties to come to power on the peaceful way.

In the bourgeois States, however, power is in the hands of the capitalists, the national businesses and cartels and multinational companies. These forces of capital have the main keys to the management of the economy and the state firmly in their hands, they make the law and through a fraudulent democratic process they appoint the government, which is under their command and acts as an official administrator of their wealth. The bourgeoisie does not safeguard its power in order to hand it over to the "Eurocommunists" but in order to protect its class interests, even with bloodshed, if necessary. To fail to see this reality, which life is confirming every day, means to close your eyes and indulge in day-dreaming. If the "Eurocommunists" do indeed succeed in gaining one or more positions in the bourgeois government they will in fact get there as representatives of capitalism, just like the other bourgeois political parties and not as representatives of the proletariat.

The bourgeois pseudo-democracy, the parliament which allegedly chooses the government, is nothing but a puppet in the hands of the power of capital which operates "behind the scenes" and dictates in various forms everything from outside. The different forms of the real power exercised "behind the scenes" get their nuances trough the various parties represented in parliament as well as the trade-unions which allegedly fight to defend the workers. In reality all the bourgeois-revisionist parties and trade-unions in the capitalist state, regardless of the names they assume, are dependent on the owning class.

Kardelj says the "Eurocommunists" are right when they link their political struggle for "socialism" with the defence of the institutions of pluralism of political forces, because, as he puts it, "...in the present situation of the countries of Western Europe, this is the only realistic road to the unity of the forces of the working class, as well as to link it with the other democratic forces of the peoples. Only this can essentially strengthen the social and political positions of the working class, i.e., make it capable of not just criticizing society but also changing it." (p. 41).

Expressing the links, solidarity and unity of the League of "Communists" of Yugoslavia with the "Eurocommunists" and all the other revisionist parties which in one way or another, in this or that form, defend capitalism and fight the revolution and true socialism, Kardelj says: "... we have reason to defend the parliamentary system and political pluralism against the attacks of the reactionary forces of bourgeois society..." (p. 61). This "ideologist" wants to say that the working class and the pseudo-communists of Western Europe are right to unite with the capitalist institutions, parliament and the bourgeois government because through this union and only in this way the working class will become capable of changing society!

From the facts mentioned above it becomes clear that the Yugoslav "self-administrative" society is for the close alliance or fusion of capitalism and socialism, because the present-day capitalists allegedly have no objection to the building of a new society in which the working class will gain the ability to fully assume its democratic "self-administrative" rights. Hence it is not difficult to understand that the author of the book recommends a transition from the "consumer society", in which the technocrats have allegedly seized power, to a "self-administrative" society in which "the individuals are associated in 'common labour' " - and this transition can be called a triumph of socialism then! There is nothing resembling genuine scientific socialism in these judgements and stands of cunning renegades. As loyal servants of the capitalist bourgeoisie, the Titoites deny the proletarian revolution and the class struggle with their writings. In claiming that the "consumer society" can be transformed into socialism gradually without violent revolution but "by the Holy Spirit" they seek to disarm the proletariat and smash its Marxist-Leninist Party.

In the capitalist countries, "reveals" Kardelj, the executive power is linked with political forces which act and impose their policy from outside parliament. Here again Kardelj is saying nothing new but simply repeating the idea as his own observation, which was expressed by Lenin in his masterful exposure of the falsity of the bourgeois democracy. It is a fine thing to assimilate and repeat Lenin's ideas, but it is neither the worry about Lenin nor Leninism that concerns Mr Kardelj. He is afraid of the "politicism" as well as of the "political monopoly" of Leninism, although it pleases him "to politicise" others and make them believe that under capitalism the executive power is really manipulated by forces outside the state organs, whereas in Yugoslavia the Presidency of the Socialist Federal Republic of Yugoslavia and the Federal Executive Council which constitutes the government, have obviously escaped this danger as if trough a miracle because they have divided the competences "in a precise manner" (p, 235). Apart from this the political strength in Yugoslavia is, according to Kardelj, concentrated in "... the delegates' assembly and moreover not just in this but in the interconnection of the assembly with the whole social structure" (p. 235). This "delegates' assembly", in regard to its "full powers and authority», reminds of the so-called councils of local self-government in the bourgeois countries, which Lenin has ridiculed saying that they

"... may be 'autonomous' only in minor matters, may be

independent only in questions of tinning washbowls." (V. I. Lenin, Collected Works, vol. 10, p. 366, Alb. ed.)

It is said that under "workers' self-administration" the "delegates" voice their opinions freely. In theory, of course, not only the "delegates" but also the workers have all rights, but in practice they enjoy none at all. In the political system of Yugoslav "self-government" everything is decided from above and nothing from below. The protests of the Yugoslav workers against the enrichment and corruption of leading officials, their demands for the elimination of economic and social distinctions, the abolition of private enterprises, restraining of political and moral corruption, protests against national discrimination etc., are well-known today. The book is full of long-drawn-out phrases which are intended to make the reader weary and thus make him believe the abstract idea that "socialist self-government exists in Yugoslavia" and that "workers' self-"administration reigns", at a time when the workers have nothing to say. The keys to the government of the country are held by the new Yugoslav bourgeoisie which operates from rightist positions while disguising itself with leftist slogans.

4. The System of Self-Administration and the Denial of the Leading Role of the Party

The Yugoslav revisionists also maintain an anti-Marxist stance towards the leading role of the communist party in the construction of socialism. According to Kardelj's "theory" the party is unable to lead any economic or administrative activity; it can and should exercise its influence only through its educational activity among the workers, so that they totally understand the socialist system.

The denial of the role of the communist party in the construction of socialism and the reduction of this role to an "ideological" and "orientating" factor is in open opposition to Marxism-Leninism. The enemies of scientific socialism substantiate this thesis by "arguing" that leadership of the party is allegedly incompatible with the decisive role which should be played by the masses of producers. Those, according to their opinion, should exercise their political influence directly and not through the communist party, because this would bring about "bureaucratic despotism"!

Contrary to the anti-scientific theses of these enemies of communism, historical experience has shown that the undivided leading role of the revolutionary party of the working class in the struggle for socialism and communism is absolutely essential. The leadership through the party constitutes a question of vital importance for the fate of the revolution and the dictatorship of the proletariat, as is well-known; it reflects a universal law of socialist revolution. Lenin says that

"… the dictatorship of the proletariat cannot be realised except through the Communist Party." (V. I. Lenin, Collected

Woks, vol. 32, p. 226, Alb. ed.)

The direct political influence of the working masses in socialist society is not in any way hampered by the communist party which represents the working class, whose interests do not run counter to the interests of the other working people. On the contrary, it is only under the leadership of the working class and its vanguard that the working masses participate broadly in governing the country and realizing their interests. In a genuine socialist country, such as Albania, the opinion of the working masses on important questions is directly sought. There are so many examples for this that they are countless, from the discussion and approval of the Constitution to the drafting of economic plans etc., etc. "Bureaucratic despotism" is a characteristic of the capitalist state and it can never be attributed to the leading role of the party under the system of the dictatorship of the proletariat, which is sternly anti-bureaucratic by its nature and class character.

Continuing the explanation of the revisionist views on the role of the party, Kardelj writes that the League of "Communists", although it must fight for the key positions of state power to be in the hands of those subjective forces which are on the side of socialism and socialist self-administration still "... cannot be a political class party" (p. 119). So this is the sort of party the Yugoslav revisionists want! They do not want and in reality do not have a political party of the working class but a bourgeois organisation, a club which anybody may enter or leave when and how it pleases him, provided only he declares he is a "communist" without needing to be such. Of course this is absolutely normal for a party like the League of "Communists" of Yugoslavia, which has nothing communist about it.

There has never been a classless party or state, nor will there ever be. The state and the parties are class products. That is how the parties and states came into existence and this is how they will be right up to communism.

Although Kardelj assumes that the leading role of the League of "Communists" has been liquidated, for demagogic purposes he still does not forget to say that this League, "through its clear stance" (which in fact is far from being clear but on the contrary obscure and blurry) "has to do a great deal to find means to solve many questions about the ways and forms for the further development of the political system of socialist self-administration". If it is not state or the party which can bring happiness to the people, as the renegade Kardelj writes, then why does he seek that these prerogatives are given to the League of "Communists" of Yugoslavia? If the Yugoslav society of "self-administration" has no need for the leadership of a single political party, as it is claimed, why then should it need the leadership of the League of "Communists" of Yugoslavia?

Whereas Marx stands for a genuine party of the working class which must lead this class and make it conscious of its historic mission, the proletariat, according to Kardelj, can carry the country forward and realise its aspirations in a spontaneous manner, even without the leading role of the party. Kardelj says this in order to justify the theory of "self-administration", this theory which stands both for political pluralism, that is, for the unity in of all social forces regardless of their ideological and social differences in the so-called Socialist League of Working People and for a party which has no communist value at all but to which he nevertheless attaches the label of the leader in the whole anti-Marxist system of "self-administration".

The revisionist Kardelj refers to the bureaucracy of the Western parties of capital. Here, too, he has discovered nothing new because it is well known that bureaucracy is part of the nature of capitalism and characteristic of it. But he denounces bureaucracy in other parties not in order to criticize them, but to hide the bureaucratization and then the liquidation of the Yugoslav communist party and the stripping of all prerogatives that belonged to it. If the Titoites place the party at the tail-end of events, phenomena, or processes of political and social life and transform it into a party of the bourgeoisie, they call this de-bureaucratisation. And in order to cover up their betrayal, they only left the name the "League of Communists of Yugoslavia" to the party.

Whether or not a party is communist, whether or not it is a party of the working class, cannot be judged from the name it bears but especially from whom it has as its leadership and what activity it carries out. Lenin said

"If a party actually is a political workers' party also depends on who leads it and what the content of its actions and its political tactic is." (V.I. Lenin, Collected Woks, vol. 31, p. 285, Alb. ed.)

And indeed the League of "Communists" of Yugoslavia did not only not escape bureaucracy but in reality it does not exist as a party of Yugoslav communists for a long time. Its swelling through numerous instruments, through a high number of bureaucratic functionaries and party officials, just like in the revisionist parties of the West or the social democratic parties, is one of the elements which cause that the League is not only no longer vanguard of the working class but even a party opposed to this class.

The rule of the proletariat and the vanguard party of this class as leader of the state and the society does not exist in Yugoslavia. According to Kardelj the League of "Communists" of Yugoslavia is in no way entitled to the political leadership in the system, because state power is "...realised through the system of delegates, while the League of Communists, as component of the self-governing system, is one of the most important elements of social influence in shaping the consciousness of the self-governing and the organs of the delegates" (p. 73). I think this needs not much explanations. What the renegade writes is enough to see for oneself that in Yugoslavia the dictatorship of the proletariat as the political rule of the working class and as state leadership of society does not exist. And since this dictatorship

60

does not exist there, there can also be no talk about the existence of the party of the working class but only of the party of the bourgeoisie.

Kardelj claims that the "one-party system" in a socialist country is a specific transformation of the bourgeois political system and the role of a party (here he refers to the Bolshevik Party) is the same "multi-party system" like in bourgeois political pluralism, with a "slight" difference, namely that in a one-party system only the leaders of this party hold all political power, while in a multi-party system the leadership changes. This imposter puts the bourgeois parties and the Bolshevik Party, which was founded by the Russian revolutionaries with Lenin heading them, on the same level. For him there is not the slightest difference between the leadership of the state and the society by the genuine party of communists and the rule of the bourgeoisie through the multi-party system. This proves once again that the Titoites, as well as the bourgeoisie, treat the political parties and the state as institutions which allegedly stand above the classes.

If it is the case that the working class is opposed to the bourgeoisie in a fight to life and death and in order to defend their antagonistic interests and to rule in society both these classes are organised in a political party, then this is not supposed to mean that the party of the working class, the Marxist-Leninist party, does not differ from the bourgeois party. On the contrary. When the Communist Party of Yugoslavia was transformed into a revisionist party, it became in no way a party standing above the classes but it it became a tool of the bourgeoisie, it only lost its proletarian class character but not its class character in general, because it was transformed into a party of the new bourgeois class. The difference between a communist party and a bourgeois party in the way of leading the state is everything else than "slight", it is very big, deep, in principle and of class nature and it cannot be reduced to the "rotation" of its leaders who hold political power, like this renegade claims.

With this "theorising" about the "slight difference"

between the bourgeois system and the socialist system and between the bourgeois party and the Marxist-Leninist Party the Yugoslav revisionists want to say that their race towards capitalism must not be seen as anything special. It is totally clear that the Yugoslav revisionists cannot take any other position in theory than the one they took in practice.

With intent to attack the construction of socialism in the Soviet Union at the times of Lenin and Stalin, Kardelj drivels about "the weak points of the one-party system": "In this system mainly the tendency of the party leadership to form a personal union with the executive state apparatus is brought to surface and this way the latter becomes a tool of technocratic-bureaucratic tendencies in society" (p.64).

In order to "escape" this "technocratic bureaucracy" and this tendency of a "personal union of the party leadership with the executive state apparatus of socialism", which they arbitrarily attribute to the Bolsheviks, the Messieurs Yugoslav revisionists have created their own system, which is nothing else but a dictatorship of the Titoite clique. In the so-called assemblies of the self-governing communities and their executive organs "... currently the bureaucratic-centrist tendencies appear very strongly" (p.232), as the author of the book admits. In Yugoslavia the executive power is manipulated by Tito and his clique. In spite of all assurances that they do not claim any power, the President of the Presidium of the League of "Communists" of Yugoslavia is the President of the Yugoslav state for life and all functionaries in the key positions of state power, the army, the economy, the foreign policy, the culture, the social organisations et al. Hold important functions on the League of "Communists" of Yugoslavia. Everything boils down to the Yugoslav revisionists, while attacking the Marxist-Leninist teachings about the leadership of the proletarian party in a socialist society, are in practice keen to hold all power in their hands. The so-called Presidency of the Socialist Federal Republic of Yugoslavia was neither created to guarantee the cooperative leadership of the state, nor to fight the bureaucracy which it relies on, nor to defend the Yugoslav state from ruling powers outside itself, as it could be heard sometimes, but as desperate attempt to secure the leadership of Titoism after Tito's death. This shows that the Yugoslav regime not only in content but also in form is nothing else but a capitalist force which suppresses the people and aims at hiding this behind treacherous phrases.

Kardelj is not able to dispose this black period in the history of Yugoslavia which was fought out on the backs of the peoples of this country; the injustices, the violence and the boundless terror which was a result of the betrayal of the leadership of the Communist Party of Yugoslavia and the construction of the Titoite dictatorship. The Titoite spokesman Kardelj tries to penetrate the darkness with some phrases to get the peoples of Yugoslavia to don't complain about their sufferings, because "our socialist revolution in its first phase, too, constituted in a certain way the one-party system of revolutionary democracy, albeit never in its 'classical' Stalinist form." (p. 64-65). This shameless renegade is not at all in the position to harm the "classical Stalinist form", which has been such a democratic and socialist form that the Tito-Kardelj-Rankovic regime can not even dream about getting close to it but that it is a shame to actually draw a comparison here. The outrageous crimes in Yugoslavia were not committed during the period of friendship with Stalin and with the Soviet union during his life time but deliberately after the break of this friendship and at the time when Yugoslavia openly took the road of "self-administration".

According to Kardelj's theory the connection of the executive organs of the League of "Communists" of Yugoslavia with the state executive organs in personal unity has been abolished "completely" and "radically" at present because the League of "Communists" of Yugoslavia has no prerogatives for the position of the leading ideological and political power in society.

In which way and what for is this kind of League then

supposed to influence the masses, if it has no prerogative for the leadership? For nothing. In a moment of desperation Tito admitted that "the League of Communists of Yugoslavia has become an unformed apolitically organisation.". But Kardelj corrects his master, in order to avoid that the Titoites completely lose their facade, and writes that allegedly "... the League of Communists of Yugoslavia has become one of the mighty pillars of democracy of the new type – the democracy of pluralism of self-governing interests." (p. 65)

If Yugoslav "self-administration" divested the League of "Communists" of Yugoslavia from political leadership, it is clear that this "self-administration" also divested the working class from its political power because the working class is only able to achieve its prerogatives through the Communist Party. If the vanguard of the class is stripped of its prerogatives then it is an absurdity to claim that the class exercises its due rights. One can imagine under those circumstances how the proletariat and the other working people are able to "self-govern" in this kind of democracy "of a new type"! Concretely Kardelj says about this question: "The League of Communists of Yugoslavia does not rule through political monopoly but is an expression of a specific but nevertheless very important form of the interests of the working class in social and historical regards and thus of the interest of all working people and of society, too – in the system of self-government and of the power of the working class and the working masses, in a system, which is based on democratic pluralism of the interests of the self-governing subjects." (p.65-66)

This overblown and confused phraseology illustrate noting else but the undeniable fact that the Party in Yugoslavia is at the tail-end, that it only exists on paper. Although Kardelj formally represents the position of strengthening the role of the party, just as he understands this role, he cannot avoid to admit: "... the League of Communists of Yugoslavia is politically and creative... in the whole system of democratic self-government and in the planning of the policies and practice of the other social and political organisations not present enough..." (p. 263-264) Where is this League present then, if not there, where it would have to be, if in Yugoslvia – as the Yugoslav news agency TANJUG lately reported – tow third of all villages lack a basic organisation of the "League of Communists". The embarrassing answer to this question is not given by Kardelj but his correct analysis of the practical actions of the League confirms without any doubt that it is nowhere present as "Party of Communists", while it can be present everywhere as party of the new Yugoslav bourgeoisie and of Tito's fascist dictatorship.

In this Yugoslav "self-administrative socialism", which Kardelj made his business to deal with theoretically, the League of "Communists" of Yugoslavia takes a specific position. This specific position, which can be found everywhere in his his book, can be interpreted as you like, that is, as specific position in the education of the working class, as specific position in the relationship towards the proletariat, as specific position in the so-called system of delegates which the League does not participate in and which must not be lead by the League for fear of "political monopoly" and other specifics. This party with these endless specific positions is entitled to have an own delegation through which they work together with the other "self-administrated" delegations at the assemblies of the so-called Socialist Alliance of Working People of Yugoslavia. This illustrates that the League of "Communists" of Yugoslavia has no independent political power and that it exercises the function of the agency of Yugoslav anarchist federalism or a long time. It exists in order to satisfy the foreign capital, which stroke roots in Yugoslavia, in order to ensure that "self-administration" will not touch the system of private property and that no party, howsoever, will change the course of this anarcho-syndicalist state.

According to E. Kardelj the role of the individual is everything in society while the working class and its party are nothing. The vanguard of the working class, he claims, is not the

Marxist-Leninist party but this vanguard consists of the "self-governing communities". This is an abstract organisation which was invented to pretend something big without really holding any life. This revisionist does not imagine the working class as the leading class of society but mingles it with all working people. The whole Yugoslav people, he says, could be seen as vanguard, in which, of course, man is put ahead of this "vanguard", man who "freely" (in the anarchist sense) expresses his goals (in this anarchist society) and realises them. From these explanations one can clearly see that the working class in Yugoslavia does not and has not acted commonly for a long time, that it has lost its leading role in Yugoslav society. Since the party and thus the power has been taken from the hands of the Yugoslav working class, it is no more a class in power, it rather got into the position of a class which is exploited by the new bourgeoisie, which rules by its manipulated state power over the working masses.

To escape the accusation that the dismissive stand towards the leading role of the party of the working class betrays the interests of this class, the notorious traitor quoted the following from the "Communist Manifesto" by Marx and Engels out of context: "The Communists do not form a separate party opposed to the other working-class parties. They have no interests separate and apart from those of the proletariat as a whole. They do not set up any sectarian principles of their own, by which to shape and mould the proletarian movement." By these quotes Kardelj wants to create the impression that Marx and Engels held the opinion that the communists need no own party as long as it is no party which differs from the other worker parties with regard to characteristics, interests and principles. What a renegade! Without a trace of diligence he regards the proletariat – through the glasses of the social democratic anti-Marxist – as an amorphous mass. He allegedly fights for general interests but has no principles, no class and no revolutionary orientation and no programme for struggle to gain his rights!

In the second chapter of the work of scientific

66

communism, in the "Manifest of the Communist Party" Marx and Engels brilliantly defined the historic mission of the communist party as an inseparable component of the working class, as its vanguard, etc., etc. but they have never promoted the opinion that the communists do not have to have an own party. On the contrary, Marx and Engels precisely wrote the Communist Manifesto, which was regarded as the first scientific programmatic document of communism, so that the communists have their own party.

5. Political-Ideological Pluralism, "Democracy" and "Socialist" Construction in Yugoslavia

Kardelj emphasises the "pluralism of the interests of the working masses" with his theory and in this pluralism he especially emphasises the role of the so-called Socialist Alliance of Working People of Yugoslavia, which is, according to him, able to unite all social forces, regardless of the ideological differences. In reality the "Socialist Alliance" is an union which only exists on paper and gets no attention in Yugoslavia. Kardelj also lets this truth slip in one place when he writes: "I do not think I exaggerate if I say that the underestimation of the social role of the Socialist Alliance... is a common attitude in the League of Communists and not only in the ranks of its members." (p.272-273). Kardelj then further illustrates the activities of this "union of all organised forces of society", like they call it in Yugoslavia, and is again forced to mention its formal character. "... The Socialist Alliance", he writes, "often solves problems only seemingly, that is, through resolutions and declarations and less in reality..." (p276). These facts Kardelj admits, which he of course only treats as weak points, are enough to undeniably prove what this lifeless alliance de facto is.

The pluralism of "socialist self-administration" expresses itself, according to Kardelj, within the "Socialist Alliance", which includes all "progressive democratic" tendencies (all tendencies, even the most regressive) in its ranks, whose representatives are enabled to discuss and decided about Yugoslavian policy. In reality nobody else but the Titoite clique decides in this front which is called pluralism of self-administrating" interests by Kardelj in order to show the Yugoslavia is not for the creation of many parties but only for one party, under the condition, that the latter is not the only power which leads society.

"... The League of Communists of Yugoslavia", says Kardelj, "bears a special political responsibility in society, a responsibility which it – of course – shares with all other socialist forces in society..." (p.74). And therefore, because responsibility is shared, there is allegedly "democratic pluralism" in Yugoslavia. So according to Kardelj "democratic pluralism", which is not the pluralism of many parties but the pluralism within the "Socialist Alliance", which also subscribes to the one-party system, is more appropriate for Yugoslavia. This idea expresses, in other words, that within the so-called Socialist Alliance the "League of Communists" and other "social and political" organisations are working, organisations which are "independent organisations... in which the League of Communists is a component which participates and works together with them..." (p.267).

Without elaborating further we can say that this "pluralism" or however one likes to call it, "democratic pluralism" or "pluralism of the interests of the working masses" or however, in reality only formally differs from bourgeois pluralism. Same as there are many parties in the capitalist system which participate in parliament and exercise influence by expressing the interests of the most important parts of the bourgeoisie or any other class, in Yugoslavia the League of "Communists" and other alliances, which do not call themselves parties but socio-political organisations exercise influence by doing their best to express the interests of the petty bourgeoisie, the labour aristocracy, etc., etc. and to maintain these interests in the capitalist Yugoslav state. The Yugoslav revisionist's conclusion that "our system is not only no one-party system, it even excludes such a system like it excludes the pluralism of many parties in bourgeois society" is an absurdity, a thesis borrowed from the anarchists and anarcho-syndicalists, which was ardently fought by Marx, Engels, Lenin and Stalin.

This theory about "political pluralism" promoted by Kardelj would also come to Hua Guofeng and Deng Xiaoping at the right time, additional to their equal rights for the different parties in the socialist state, the mutual control, etc.

As Kardelj brags about institutions for development in the political system of "socialist self-administration" he cannot avoid – in order not to over-egg the pudding – to admit there are also exaggerations, mistakes and defects because: " The new conditions are still not yet realised in a satisfying way and still not yet work in a satisfying way in many categories." (p.26) But even if he would not admit that, Yugoslav reality proves on a daily base that "self-administration" has come to a dead-end street and therefore his consolatory explanations which refer to the "self-administration" as "the most qualified socialist system" are not believed by those who know Yugoslavia and its political system from close up.

The political system of "self-administration" in Yugoslavia is an impertinent disguise of the revisionist betrayal of Marxism-Leninism, of scientific socialism and of communism. As anti-Marxists the Yugoslav Titoites have never been and are not in favour of the construction of socialism but for the immortalisation of capitalism in various forms. Unable to stop the process of the decay of capitalist social order, they try to invent many various "theories" in order to at least slow it down. According to the Yugoslav revisionists every people, every state is able to construct socialism without having to rely on universal laws and principles, without Marxist-Leninist ideology. They do not admit that socialism is one single economic and social system but claim that allegedly there can be various forms of socialism. They misuse and twist the Marxist-Leninist thesis about the creative application of the ideology of the working class under the specific conditions of each country if they insist that no universal laws for all countries for the construction of socialism are existing and moreover that every country is able and allowed to construct a "socialism" different from other countries according to its own wishes and in its own way.

Now, with regard to socialist construction, we have to

take the concrete conditions of every country into consideration but in every single country socialism can only be constructed on the basis of Marxism-Leninism, on the basis of the universal laws and principles in all countries, which cannot be passed over if one does not want to end at capitalism again, like Yugoslavia.

To "substantiate" the thesis that every country has to construct its specific socialism the Yugoslav revisionists, which Kardelj represents, say that "socialist self-administration cannot be forced upon the bourgeois democracies of Western Europe or upon American democracy, for example" because they allegedly have not achieved the same conditions as Yugoslavia. According to them socialism is achievable as well through the political pluralism of the Western parliamentarian system as without the latter. So every country is able to construct its specific socialism, without any experience, yes even without the theory of scientific socialism by Marx and Engels. And still, they think, praising "self-administration" as the best system of the whole world, that this system, regardless of the specific path every country chooses for the construction of socialism, can be adopted and realised on a worldwide level .

Lead by his subjectivism and his rampant passion which aims against the experience of the socialist construction in the Soviet Union at the time of Lenin and Stalin, Kardelj raves so badly against this experience and completely loses his ability to judge that he labels this experience as a reactionary process and puts it on the same level as the political pluralism of European kind. He expresses it this way: "Therefore the attempts to force, for example, the political pluralism of European kind upon nations where neither the conditions nor the need for such a system exists, in fact play the same reactionary role in the current social processes as the attempts to force this or that 'model' of socialism upon those countries who do neither have the conditions nor the need for such a model." (p.49)

This whole tirade is nothing but a play on words with the single goal to degrade Marxism-Leninism and the universal laws of the construction of the socialist society, to fool the masses and to eternalise the capitalist system by giving it various "socialist" appearances. This is the reason that Kardelj talks not even once about the actual destruction of the power of the capital in his book titled "Directions of the Development of the Political System of Socialist Self-Administration".

According to this Yugoslavian "great ideologist" the political pluralism of bourgeois parliamentarianism is a system which transforms the individual into an "abstract-political citizen", which makes them passive and keeps them from being an exponent of certain concrete human or social interests. In Yugoslavia, in contrast, the citizen allegedly does not run the risk to be transformed into an "abstract-political citizen" because "self-administration" allegedly teaches him to defend his won interests in the first instance! This thesis, too, is as far away from the truth as Kardelj's other theses. His "politicized" citizen in the capitalist countries is not twiddling his thumbs. In those countries they are denied their rights and the laws of capital have cut off the way for the defense of the interests of the working masses but still the workers try and struggle to break the chains of capitalist slavery. To deny this struggle the working class leads in capitalism stands in opposition to the facts.

In the capitalist social order not all people conform to the bourgeois policy and the norms of bourgeois morals. On the contrary, not only that the predominant majority of the members of capitalist society – the proletariat and the other exploited and oppressed working masses – do not conform to the bourgeois policy and morals, they even oppose themselves to them and and fight them in various forms and by many means. This surely didn't escape Kardelj but he twists the facts in order to get an affirmation that the individual, the human, the citizen allegedly takes the main part in his "specific socialism" and is not "politicized" by the party, that this concrete individual is able to defend its concrete interests easily in the political system of "self-administration", and only in this system! If one consequently

72

follows Kardelj's train of thought till the end and according to his own logic than one has to accept the absurdity that more than a million of unemployed people, who exist and starve in Yugoslavia, are not suffering this fate due to the system of "self-administration" but due to their own carelessness because they just did not want to defend their concrete interests! In "socialist self-administration" Yugoslavia the working masses have been that much politically disarmed that they are no longer in the position to even defend their most general interests. In their overwhelming majority they have become people who only worry about keeping their job or, if they have none, to find a job in order to earn a living in and outside the country. In reality only few workers are interested what this "system of self-administration", this "united work", this "democratic pluralism" etc. are. This is one of the goals the Titoites were aiming for since the invention of "self-administrative socialism", precisely that the working masses will care about defending their rights as little as possible, that they are interested as little as possible in politics, that they only see their narrow self-interests and disregard the collective class interest.

In the system of bourgeois parliamentarianism the working class is inevitably "politicized", according to Kardelj, because syndicalism and trade union struggle alone does not secure the way to political power. Further he writes that such "politicizing" separates the working class into parties and therefore, according to his opinion, the new danger arises that the "party bureaucracy" will be active in the name of the class.

It is true that the struggle within the limits of trade unions will not secure political power for the working class in the capitalist countries, therefore the workers organize themselves in political parties in order to defend the interests of their class. But Kardelj's foremost care is not the exposure of syndicalism and not of the different "workers'" parties either which are created in the West and with which the Yugoslav revisionists are allied. Instead he wants to show that from bourgeois parliamentarianism and the bourgeois parties up to the others, the communist and revisionist parties and the trade unions, all separate the workers in an equal way, which is why those parties, according to him, have to be liquidated. The bourgeoisie and the revisionist are not angry with their friend because of this position because they understand very well that Kardelj only means the liquidation of the genuine Marxist-Leninist parties by this while the other parties of the bourgeoisie may continue to exist because this parties, both when they are just one or two and when they are numerous, are no obstacle in the transformation of the capitalist order to the "socialist order"!

One must not be surprised about the fact that Kardelj writes "in theory" about a question while in practice everything looks very different. Behind the theorizing he practices the charlatan hides the numerous manipulations which took place in Yugoslavia in order to transform this society, which at the beginning adopted in some respects an allegedly socialist orientation only in order to mask itself, into a capitalist society. Although Kardelj is not consequent because of the positions he represents and therefore cannot be consequent, he is in fact for the bourgeois parliamentarian system which he necessarily has to present as different from the Yugoslavian "specific" system. His inconsistency becomes obvious when he does not completely reject this system but calls it democratic, a system in which "... the working class and all other democratic forces play an important progressive role in struggling for the consolidation of the position of the parliament in society and for the expansion of its competences in comparison to the forces of the non-parliamentarian powers." (p.55)

This "theorizing" by Kardelj aims not at all at the exposure of the tendencies which can be found in the current development of the capitalist state, namely that the executive (the government) expands it competences more and more at the expense of the legislative (the parliament) and thus creates the conditions for the installation of fascism in case the monopoly bourgeoisie considers this as necessary. Kardelj is not at all worried about the danger of increasing fascism which threatens many capitalist states today because his state, too, takes the same path. Therefore he demands that the working class does not achieve its historic mission – overthrowing the power of the bourgeoisie by the revolution, like Marx and Lenin taught us. When he writes in favour of bourgeois parliamentarianism Kardelj unintentionally reveals that the Titoites are exposed to strong pressure especially from the American and the Western European capital, which invested in Yugoslavia. This pressure is supposed to develop bourgeois democracy in a broader scale in Yugoslavia, so that there are many parties created in this country: social democratic, revisionist, "communist" and others. Now the Yugoslav revisionists are not opposed to the parliamentarian multi-party system but they still don't want to destroy their own one-party system which they propagated as "self-governed", not only because they would be finally exposed but because they are afraid of the danger that this the monopoly of the Titoites might be challenged in all state affairs – their monopoly in the army, in the UDBA and in their other repressive organs as well as in their traitorous organs for the bourgeois manipulation of the people.

In reality Kardelj does not reject what he calls "political monopoly" in governing the society and about which he claims is a privilege of the bosses of the political parties and the executive organs of bourgeois "democracy". So he does not reject the parliamentarian and the non-parliamentarian system but condemns "the remains of this system" which socialism allegedly inherits in its initial and early phase.

It shall be understood that Kardelj, without attacking the form of the bourgeois parliament, makes the attempt to compare the former with the state organs of a genuine socialist society. These ideas are revealed even more clearly when he writes that basically the bourgeois parliament is the same without "self-government" as the political one-party system of socialism which lacks the "etatist form of social property". By political system "in the etatist form of social property" Kardelj refers to our people's councils as well as the Soviet power which was constructed by Lenin in the Soviet Union in order to build the new socialist society under the leadership of the Bolshevik Party.

By rejecting the aims of the October Revolution and the enormous work, which was done in the Soviet Union for many years under the leadership of Lenin and later Stalin in order to build socialism, the revisionist Kardelj wants to prove that Yugoslavia, which liquidated the "etatist" social property and transformed it to "socialised property", did not betray socialism, as he is accused of, but allegedly invented a "socialist" state, a "self-administrative socialism" which in theory Kardelj does not recommend to everybody but hopes with all his hearts that everybody will follow it in practice.

At present the "one-party system" in Yugoslavia does, according to Kardelj, confirms no more to the model of "specific socialism". While the latter was originally introduced to the development of the socialist revolution as an element of the initial structure of the dictatorship of the proletariat, now it must be called "... incompatible with the socio-economic and democratic relations of socialist self-administration and the democratic pluralism of the interests of self-government". (p.63)

The Yugoslav revisionists act as if they did not agree with the rule of multiple parties in the bourgeois society but also do not want to accept the leadership of the state and the society by a single party of the working class. Therefore they pretend as if they had discovered the "golden mean" in form of the so-called "democratic pluralism". It is true that the Yugoslav system of "self-government" contains both, elements of the "one-party system" as well as elements of the "multi-party system". But this obscure system is nothing else than a capitalist system, an evil spawn of the Yugoslavian bourgeoisie in order to rule over the working masses and to disguise themselves behind a "Marxist" facade.

In order to throw dirt at Lenin and Stalin the Titoite author tries to contrast these great leaders of the world proletariat with each other to "demonstrate" that they allegedly had not the same conception of the political system of the socialist state. And his is the way he slanders them: "Between Lenin's and Stalin's conception of the political system of the socialist state there is a massive irreconcilability. Basis and nature of Lenin's conception of the Soviet power is direct democracy..." (p.67)

It is common knowledge that Stalin was an eager pupil, a loyal comrade and a very close assistant of Lenin. To this day nobody but the enemies have dared to to oppose Stalin to Lenin. By these hints a hostile goal is pursued nut the international communist and workers movement is accustomed to such maneuvers by the revisionists who declared once that they are Marxist-Leninists but "Anti-Stalinists" and now try to oppose Lenin to Marx and argue whether they should call themselves only "Marxists" or maybe still "Leninists" after all. And tomorrow they will drop their masks of revisionists and renegades and will firmly declare that they are also opposed to Marx. They will invent suitable "theories" for this step, too, which will be anything but communist and proletarian.

As true Marxist Lenin talked about socialist democracy, about the direct participation of the working masses in the state affairs of the country and realised these revolutionary ideas for several years, when he lead the Soviet state. After him Stalin followed the same way. But Lenin had in no way the weakening of the state of the dictatorship of the proletariat and the leading role of the Bolshevik Party in mind when he talked about socialist democracy and direct participation of the working masses in the state affairs. He never contrasted the dictatorship of the proletariat to true democracy, which he defined as the state which

"... is democratic in a new way (for the proletariat and the propertyless in general) and dictatorial in a new way (for the bourgeoisie)." (V.I. Lenin, Collected Woks, vol. 25, p. 488, Alb.

77

ed.)

This illustrates very clearly that Lenin was never in favour and could have never been in favour of replacing the dictatorship of the bourgeoisie by this or that system of "self-administration", invented by the Yugoslav revisionists in order to return to capitalism.

In Lenin's and Stalin's times the working class was in power in the Soviet Union and successfully led, planned and realised the task of the socialist construction through the Bolshevik Party. In Yugoslavia the big role of the socialist state has been disregarded and it has been identified with the so-called "system of delegates", which, as Kardelj admits, "... features sever weak points in all directions of its functioning." (p.213)

Kardelj himself understands that the reference to Lenin regarding the question of democracy cannot help him to justify the "system of self-government" in the least. Therefore he tries to make people believe by sophisms that Lenin's conception "... is not worked out to its factual consequences... but it is obvious that its nature is direct democracy, that is, the system of self-government." (p.67) Kardelj "philosophises" and due to a lack of arguments he tries to compensate by arbitrary and fantastic interpretations. He intends to make people believe that Lenin initially correctly represented the idea of "self-government" but later he lacked the opportunity to develop it further in such a way which would be convenient for Tito and Kardelj. The view expressed by Lenin, that the proletariat will lead and organise the Soviet power and rule the country through its party, was and still remains the basis of the Marxist-Leninist theory. Exactly this crucial question of theoretical and practical importance is avoided by the Titoites and they seek to cover up this deviance by twisting Lenin's correct theses.

In the opinion of the Titoites Stalin had "... a concept of indirect democracy, i.e., in core he adopted the classical political system of the bourgeois state and its political pluralism, only that he intended the role of the multi-party system in the bourgeois parliamentarian state for one single party." (p.68) The Titoites argue that Stalin allegedly deviated from the Leninist conception because he implemented an "indirect democracy" by leading the state through a party very similar to the bourgeois parties and by other elements of the parliamentarian system. This is this pseudo-Marxist's devastating criticism of the activities and the work of Joseph Stalin! Stalin sees, like Lenin, democracy from the angle of class, as a form of the political organisation of society, as a political precondition for the involvement of the masses in the government of the country, to defend and consolidate the dictatorship of the proletariat and to block the way for revisionist degeneracy and the restoration of capitalism. As the Marxist-Leninist he was, Stalin was vehemently against any one-sided, liberal and anarchist grasp of democracy and took a firm stand against the petty bourgeois signs of disintegration and speculations with the rights and liberties the proletarian democracy guarantees. And he was very well advised to do so. The revisionists in contrast want to turn the proletarian democracy into a bourgeois democracy in theory, too, like they already did in practice. And that is exactly why they are opposed to Stalin.

The excuse the Yugoslav pseudo-Marxists use to justify their criticism of the genuine socialist system is that allegedly the meaning of the terms "worker" and "working class" has changed today that the conception of the term "citizen" has changed, too. According to them "the working class has become an abstract political subject which does not exercise any power but in whose name power can be exercised". So this means that in a true socialist system not the working class exercises power but somebody else who rules over the class in their name. This is a big fraud, a shameless distortion of reality. This means being based on the philosophical positions of idealism and to see the truth not in objective facts but in what goes around in your mind.

The revisionist Kardelj derives from this the idea that the

worker is concretely worth nothing in the relations of production of the socialist social order, in his relations to the other workers, in his social position and so on! And in his opinion this is allegedly how "... the dogmatism of social property as state property and therefore the necessity for a centralist state as well as the leading role of the state and party apparatus arises... while the class interests and the efforts of the concrete worker... are discredited, respectively called as acts outside of the common legality..." (p.70)

So this is how Kardelj twists the true socialist system and the socialist relations of production at the time of Lenin and Stalin and thus the whole construction of socialism on our country. By militating against democratic centralism, the leading role of the party, the state form of socialist property etc., Kardelj wants to illustrate "the superiority" of "the system of self-administration" but in reality he unmasks himself by placing himself openly above the eternal ideas of the classics of Marxism-Leninism, above these basic question. In fact his "accusations" against us transform into confessions which turn against the Yugoslav political "self-administrative system". Today Yugoslav reality proves on a daily basis and will prove this even better tomorrow where Tito's clique and Kardelj's Yugoslavia is leading its peoples and its working class.

The Titoites claim their system was "self-administrative". But who are those, who govern themselves in Yugoslavia? The workers or the peasants? Neither the workers nor the peasants. They are just as oppressed as their comrades in the capitalist countries. In the "system of self-administration" those rule who are at the top of pyramid, the new bourgeoisie, who, while labelling themselves "communists", oppress the people and are in reality nothing else but bourgeois technocrats who lead the bureaucratic, etatist and fascist power. The "delegates' assemblies", the executive state organs in the system of delegates, etc., consist of such elements.

In the system of the dictatorship of the proletariat the

mass organisation take up a special position, as is widely known and play an important role. They are levers of the party to connect itself with the masses and to realise the political rule of the working class and socialist democracy. The social organisation in socialism makes the line of the proletarian party accessible to the people, they are an enormous weapon of the revolution and of socialist construction, they are fighting tribunes where the public opinion asserts itself. They have the task to educate the masses and and to make them conscious and able to actively participate in the socialist construction and the government business.

The tasks which these organisations hold as a component of the system of the dictatorship of the proletariat are performed under the leadership of the party of the working class within the limits of their own characteristics and specifics.

The social organisations cannot be effective if they are isolated from the proletarian party, from the other organisations and from the socialist state. If one would assume the opposite then it would be theoretically senseless that they are elements of a single system, they would be transformed into dead organisms in practice, without any function and without fulfilling any tasks for the benefit of the socialist order of society.

Just like the party and the state, the mass organisations in Yugoslavia have been treated and judged from an outright anarchist position. In contrast to Lenin's idea that the mass organisations

"... are the closest and most essential assistants of the state power..." (V.I. Lenin, Collected Woks, vol. 33, p. 202, Alb. ed.)

the idea has been promoted in Yugoslavia that the cooperation of these organisations with the socialist state was a form of "bureaucratic etatsim". The Yugoslav revisionists imagine that all of these these organisations are able to act independently from the party. "We", Kardelj says, "have departed from the world view according to which these organisations have been so-called transmission belts of the League of Communists for a long time." (p.267) Here there is no talk at all about the only party in Yugoslavia and the Yugoslavian state, which are both in the hands of the bourgeoisie, exercising no power on these organisations. On the contrary, the Titoites never went without the manipulation of the masses by the social organisations but Kardelj is getting at something else by this statement. He just wants to destroy he connection of the Marxist-Leninist parties with the masses while the whole revolutionary experience shows that these parties need those organisations, lead by the proletarian party in order to create and hold up genuine connections with the organised masses.

It is a well known fact that the idea of the leading role of the Marxist-Leninist party is closely connected to the idea of its revolutionary ideology. To detach the mass organisation from the party therefore means to detach them from the Marxist-Leninist ideology and and to close the thus created gap by the bourgeois revisionist ideology. This intention is revealed clearly when Kardelj writes about the human as a member of the "Socialist Alliance": "... it cannot be said that his view will always and in all regards be according to the ideology of Marxism." (p.280) This means that the Yugoslav worker is also allowed to follow bourgeois, feudal, fascist and other ideas and ideologies and will further be supported by the Titoite regime in his ideological confusion.

The fact that mass organisations are an inherent part of the system of the dictatorship of the proletariat does not mean that they will become to "partners" or "appendices" of the state apparatus under the mask of democracy and by giving them some "state" competences, like it was the case in the revisionist Soviet Union. The genuine party of the working class which loyally keeps to Marxism-Leninism has to take care that the role of the social organisations does not fade but is always strengthened further. In Yugoslavia, Kardelj writes, the phenomenon can be detected that the basic organisations of the trade unions "... have become the tail of those organs which govern work." (p.295) This happened because the role of the social organisations, their place in society and the relations they have to maintain towards the party and the state have been defined from twisted positions.

Kardelj's book puts especial emphasis on the "Socialist Alliance of Working People", on the trade unions, on the "Socialist Youth League", etc., about which one could write a good many and polemicize for a long time. But we did not go into the full particulars here because we think it is better to outline only the principle deviances of the Yugoslav revisionists in regard to organisation, the aims and actions of mass organisations.

The Yugoslav revisionists also take a reactionary stance on the role of religion and its ideology. It is a well known fact that the religious ideology always serves and helps the exploiting classes to rob and oppress the working masses. It is a tool to breed the feeling of helplessness in humans in the face of the suffering, the misfortune and the misery. The religious ideology clouds the human mind and paralyses their will for the transformation of nature and society. This is why Marx, as is well-known, compared religion to opium. He wrote: "Religion is the sigh of the oppressed creature, the heart of a heartless world, and the soul of soulless conditions. It is the opium of the people."

Precisely because of the reactionary role religion plays it enjoyed and enjoys the support of the ruling classes. The language of the capitalist the revisionist and the reactionary clergyman is essentially the same. The Marxist-Leninist party cannot arrange itself with the religious ideology and its influence. The theoretical basis of the policy and of the programme of the true party of the working class is the Marxist-Leninist philosophy and not idealism and religion. The class struggle for the construction of socialism cannot be separated from the struggle against religion.

In Yugoslavia religion was judged and treated in just the

same way as in the other capitalist states, there is absolutely no difference here. The poisoning of the masses by the ideology of religion is seen as nothing but a personal matter and the party and the state placidly watch this happening because for them religion is: "... never an obstacle for the equal integration of the religious citizen in the socialist life of society." (p.178) One sees what a fine kind of socialism this is: the religious idea in no way stands in opposition to this socialism and, as Kardelj writes: "For the overwhelming majority of religious workers socialism has become a matter of their deepest conviction..." (p.179-180) Now we hear this "great philosopher" claim that the clerics with their deep idealistic and religious beliefs have suddenly fallen in love with socialism, with the social order which is based on the Marxist-Leninist philosophy, on dialectical and historical materialism. Not only the workers, the communists and every honest person on this planet will wonder while reading these phrases of the Titoite renegade but also the clerics themselves will laugh because till this day they have not even dreamed about claiming that the like socialism, this socialism which they cursed and still wholeheartedly curse. By their reconciliation with the religious ideology the Yugoslav revisionists prove even further how "Marxist" they are, how "materialist" their ideology and this how socialist the political system of "self-administration" is, which is based upon their ideology.

The Party of Labour of Albania has consequently applied the Marxist-Leninist teaching on the state of the dictatorship of the proletariat and on socialist democracy, on the leading and undivided role of the party of the working class and on the necessity of unfolding class struggle. Our historical reality confirms in an impressing way that, if the universal laws of Marxism-Leninism are applied while taking the specific conditions of the country into consideration, revolution is victorious and the process of the construction of the socialist society cannot be stopped. The example of Albania refutes all "theorising" of the capitalist and revisionist philosophers against the dictatorship of the proletariat, against the leading role of the party and against the unfolding of the class struggle.

We mainly owe our great victories at the front of the socialist construction to the loyalty to Marxism-Leninism. If we always triumphed over our enemies that is because we have remained true to our principles because we have been honest and brave revolutionaries.

It is because the Marxist-Leninist theory is realised in the practice of socialist construction in Albania that this practice has become a target for the attacks from this theory's opponents.

When it is a matter of defending Marxist-Leninist principles, we will bravely deal with the enemies of our ideology, because we cannot stop halfway or make foul compromises like those the capitalists and revisionists want to force upon us.

The struggle between the Marxist-Leninists and the traitors against the ideology of the proletariat carries on and will be carrying on for so long until revisionism, which arises and develops as an agency of the bourgeoisie and of imperialism, has been done away with. It is our duty as Marxist-Leninists to defend the revolutionary ideology of the working class. Under the current circumstances that duty has become even more obligatory, now that Chinese revisionism has been added to the old revisionism. The successful achievement of this task demands that we recognise, analyse and unveil the anti-Marxist counter-revolutionary theories and practices of the enemies who have been attacking especially the Marxist teaching on the dictatorship of the proletariat and the party of the new type under the slogans of the "creative development of Marxism" and the "struggle against dogmatism".

The socialist society is strengthened by the struggle against its enemies, that is why we communists have to lead this struggle frontally until we have gained victory. We are revolutionaries and defend the socialist economic and social order which is the new and most progressive order on the whole world whereas the revisionists are reactionary because they kneel to the old bourgeois order and capitulate to it. The future looks dark for our enemies and blissful for us. But this future does not arrive on its own, one has to prepare its way continuously and diligently by struggling on in the fields of politics, ideology, economy, in the field of the defence, etc.

Like many other books published by the international bourgeoisie and by international revisionism, in order to propagate their reactionary, anti-Marxist and anti-Leninist ideas, Kardelj's book has to be exposed for what it is so that the communists, the workers and the progressive persons who either do not know revisionist reality or who know it only from afar, are not misled by the "leftist" slogans. In order to sharpen our watchfulness, to stand at the summit of our mission as communists, we must remember Lenin's important statement:

"People always ... (will be) the foolish victims of deception and self-deception in politics... until they have learnt to seek out the interests of some class or other behind all moral, religious, political and social phrases, declarations and promises." (V.I. Lenin, Collected Woks, vol. 19, p. 9, Alb. ed.)

www.ingramcontent.com/pod-product-compliance
Lightning Source LLC
Chambersburg PA
CBHW060159290526
45789CB00003B/1082